The Jossey-Bass Nonprofit & Public Management Series also includes:

Tools for Innovators

Tools for Innovators

Creative Strategies for Managing Public Sector Organizations

Steven Cohen

William Eimicke

Jossey-Bass Publishers • San Francisco

Substantial discounts on bulk quantities of Jossey-Bass books are available to corporations, professional associations, and other organizations. For details and discount information, contact the special sales department at Jossey-Bass Inc., Publishers (415) 433-1740; Fax (800) 605-2665.

For sales outside the United States, please contact your local Simon & Schuster International Office.

www.josseybass.com

Manufactured in the United States of America on Lyons Falls Turin Book. This paper is acid-free and 100 percent totally chlorine-free.

Chapter 3: Excerpts, including definition of "reengineering" by Michael Hammer and James Champy. Copyright © 1993 by Michael Hammer and James Champy. Reprinted by permission of HarperCollins Publishers, Inc.

Chapter 7: Quotes and paraphrases by D. Osborne/T. Gaebler, *Reinventing Government*, (pages 87, 92). Copyright © 1992 by David Osborne and Ted Gaebler. Reprinted with permission of Addison Wesley Longman.

Library of Congress Cataloging-in-Publication Data

Cohen, Steven, date.
  Tools for innovators : creative strategies for managing public sector organizations / Steven Cohen, William Eimicke.
    p. cm. — (Jossey-Bass nonprofit and public management series)
  Includes bibliographical references (p. 204) and index.
  ISBN 0-7879-0953-X
  1. Organizational change.   2. Organizational change—Case studies.
3. Public administration.   4. Public administration—Case studies.
I. Eimicke, William B.   II. Title.   III. Series.
JF1525.O73C65   1998   97-51284
352.3'67—dc21

FIRST EDITION
HB Printing 10 9 8 7 6 5 4 3 2 1

The Jossey-Bass
Nonprofit and Public Management Series

Contents

Exhibits

To Donna and Karen

Preface

As the twenty-first century begins, organizations find themselves under enormous stress. Communication, computer, and transportation technology have helped to generate a highly competitive world economy. Old stable bureaucracies that seemed permanent have been attacked, modified, and at times replaced. Smaller, more agile, less hierarchical, multinational networks of organizations are now involved in creating the goods, services, and public programs on which we depend. In the public sector, government officials are being challenged to demonstrate that they can deliver effective and efficient services and regulation.

Public administration used to mean the management of governmental bureaucracies. Though that was complicated enough, the world of public management has gotten far more complex. Today's public administrator must manage a complex set of interorganizational relationships spanning governments, nonprofit organizations, and private firms. Moreover, in a global economy the cost of government itself can dramatically affect the competitiveness of a nation, a state, or a locality's private sector. Government that is fat, lazy, and inefficient is more than an inconvenience; it can be a significant drag on a local economy.

Today's public manager must do more than be the effective manager of an agency's internal operations. Effectiveness is a necessary but not sufficient condition for success; today's public manager must be a creative innovator as well. The purpose of this book is to introduce public sector professionals to the tools that today's most innovative managers are using to bring about change in their organizations.

This book tells you what these tools are all about, how to use them, their costs and benefits, and perhaps most critical, how to use them together. All of the tools discussed in this book have been written about in separate books, and frequently the authors who write about innovation tools take the approach of tool advocates. Although we understand the intellectual enthusiasm for a new tool (Cohen and Brand, 1993), it is important to demythologize these tools and learn how to integrate them within a single framework of management innovation. That is the aim of this book. A new tool is nice, but once you get used to the new high-powered drill, it is time to rediscover the importance of the hammer and the saw. A craftsperson must learn how to apply tools when appropriate to the task at hand. In this book we introduce you to each innovation tool and then demonstrate in three case studies how other public managers have attempted to innovate using these tools. Many of the lessons we discuss in these chapters we learned through direct experience. We hope that both you and we can learn from these successes and failures.

Tools of Public Management

The field of management is typically characterized by the "flavor of the month"—the most recent management practice or fad that has captured the imagination of managers, consultants, and academics. The new management innovation is presented independently and is touted as a silver bullet—the answer to the difficult problems of managing human behavior in organizations. We have written this book to review the latest practices and to integrate them into a comprehensive approach to managing organizations. We conceptualize all of these management practices—from TQM to human resource management, from budgeting to reengineering—as essential tools for public managers.

We have made an analytic distinction in this book between the tools we term traditional functional tools and those that we consider innovation tools. Traditional functional management tools include what have also been termed reporting and control structures: budgeting, human resource management, information management, and organizational structure. Strategic planning is sometimes seen as a traditional functional tool and we have written about it as such. However, it is so central that we have also included it in our discussion of innovation tools. Traditional functional tools are at least as necessary to the effective operation of organizations as are the newer innovation tools, and we have written about these tools in our previous works (Cohen, 1988; Cohen and Eimicke, 1995).

The innovation tools we examine in this book are strategic planning, reengineering, Total Quality Management, benchmarking and performance management, team management, and privatization. We have written previously about strategic planning and Total Quality Management (Cohen and Kamieniecki, 1991; Cohen and Brand, 1993). In our earlier work we devoted attention to media and community relations, the public sector fields that are analogous to marketing in the private sector (Cohen, 1988; Cohen and Eimicke, 1995). To date we have not found an innovation tool that advances the work we discussed earlier. Perhaps the growth of the Internet and the World Wide Web will lead to such a tool, but at the moment we find no analogous innovative communication tools.

Leadership is another ubiquitous management tool that we do not discuss in this work. For our views on the subject we refer you to our discussion in *The New Effective Public Manager* (Cohen and Eimicke, 1995). The emphasis in the present work is not on leadership, communication, and public participation, but we do consider these areas crucial. We plan to provide a more detailed treatment of innovation in these areas in a later work.

The distinction between traditional functional management tools and management innovation tools is a significant manifestation of changing conceptions of the meaning, purpose, and work of management. In its prebureaucratic formulation, management was imbedded in a somewhat mystical concept of familial, tribal, or national leadership in which authority was nonrationally based on mysticism, heredity, fear, awe, might, or some combination of those factors. With the development of representative democracy and bureaucracy, the basis of authority shifted to social contracts and evolved into what we now call a rational basis. Nevertheless, traditional bureaucratic management was about direction, control, reporting the results of control efforts, and then rearranging control structures to ensure compliance with management direction.

This brand of prototypical management results in budgets, personnel systems, financial accounting and reporting systems, management by objectives, and accompanying information systems (that is, nonfinancial reporting systems). Again, these are the management tools we characterize as traditional functional tools. They evolved from a mass production mode of management, characteristic of the early and mid-twentieth century.

With the growth of postindustrial, information, and service-based economies, the demands placed on management and organizations have changed. In part cause and in part effect, members of organizations have achieved higher educational levels than in the past and are more apt to expect organizational life to provide them with mental stimulation and collegiality. Employees are no longer willing to check their brains at the door when they come to work. Individuals have begun to perceive themselves as empowered professionals and expect to have meaningful input into the management decision-making process. In addition, managers increasingly have taken on the role of facilitators, coordinators, and simulators. For both workers and managers to fulfill these new roles within an organization, the old tools of control and reporting structures must be augmented.

Modern managers require internal tools, such as team processes and performance measurement with relevance to workers, as well as management and TQM. People in organizations cannot simply be ordered around anymore. In a rapidly changing environment, organizations must be capable of great agility and rapid change. Consequently they must be able to tap into the brainpower of their staff. Innovation tools help them to do this.

Sometimes the demands of a rapidly changing external environment precipitate changes that exceed the response capacity of the current organization's members. This effect requires externally oriented innovation tools such as privatization (or contracting out), reengineering, and benchmarking. Traditional functional tools do not help managers when the current configuration of organizational capacity proves insufficient to undertake a changing mission. The new world of organizational management requires a new kind of manager—a creative public manager capable of utilizing both traditional and innovative management tools.

The Creative Public Manager

Management is a craft, not a science. It requires analogies rather than algorithms. Yet it is a craft and not an art form. Management exists to get a job done, and not for its own sake. A dynamic, fast-paced environment requires the manager to use creativity and innovation to practice the management craft effectively. Managers do not innovate because it is cutting-edge or "modern" but because it is essential for their organizations' survival.

Although change and creativity are necessary, the challenges of innovation should not be minimized. Our understanding of complex organizations has taught us that change and organizational learning are difficult processes. The risk of failure is great. Misdirection, lack of focus, and collapse are dangers for any organization that attempts too much innovation and spins out of control. We are cautious enough to prefer organizational stagnation to an innovation implosion. Our overriding concern for management effectiveness leads us to explore systematically what we call innovation tools.

The goal of this book is to demythologize emerging innovation techniques. We try to bring them down to earth by conceptualizing them as tools. We then provide an operating manual to illustrate how they work. We examine their benefits and their costs, and we consider the conditions under which they tend to be most and least useful. The second section of the book provides concrete case examples of successful innovation efforts. Each success story includes failures as well, so we make the point that even the best innovation efforts are often a case of two steps forward and one step back.

We believe in appropriate management technology. A manager should use the tools most suitable to the job at hand. Our experience in management has taught us that the most effective techniques are often simple and easy to use. Tools become easier to use as the practitioner gains experience with them. Our hope, however, is that this book will encourage managers to take risks with unfamiliar innovation techniques so they will become experienced in those techniques and add them to their palette of management tools.

Overview of the Book

The book describes six key public sector management innovation tools and presents three case studies of efforts to apply those tools: in government, in a nonprofit organization, and in a private firm implementing a public program. Chapter One defines the concept

of public management innovation and discusses the book's overall approach. This chapter develops an overall framework for
assessing management innovation techniques that delineates their
characteristics and assesses their utility in specific situations. The
framework focuses on a single, key issue: What is the purpose of
management innovation, or what are we trying to change? The
chapter's framework for analyzing the use of management innovation tools includes three elements: the definition and characteristics of the tool itself, the organization's internal social structure
and operational capacities, and the organization's environment.

The chapters in Part One, Chapters Two through Seven, present six of the most widely used public sector management innovation tools: strategic planning, reengineering, Total Quality
Management (TQM), benchmarking and performance measurement, team management, and privatization. In each chapter we
define the tool, describe how it works, and address the benefits,
costs, and challenges of using it.

The chapters in Part Two, Chapters Eight through Ten, present a series of case studies of public sector innovation. These case
studies provide examples of the challenges faced by managers as
they attempt to innovate. The chapters discuss how innovations are
introduced and adjusted to the specific needs of real-world situations. Organizations that are serious about using these tools end
up going through a period of trial and error as they tailor them to
meet their unique needs. Each case involves an innovation effort
that we have been involved in as consultants.

Chapter Eight describes how the New York City Department of
Parks and Recreation has used TQM, privatization, and performance measurement to manage a very large park system with
declining fiscal resources. Chapter Nine examines innovation in
the nonprofit sector and looks at the lessons learned by the Indianapolis Private Industry Council (IPIC). IPIC used strategic planning, reengineering, privatization, and an enhanced customer
orientation to transform itself from a moderately effective employment and training provider into a national expert in community
workforce development.

Chapter Ten looks at America Works, a private firm that provides job training and places welfare recipients in jobs. America
Works performs a public policy function that could be in government and that is paid for by government but that is organized as a

private, profit-seeking firm. America Works adopted a team approach to management in 1996 and 1997 and thereby dramatically improved its job placement rate. The chapter describes its experience with team management and is a case study of the evolution and development of a firm involved in a privatized government function.

The book's Conclusion summarizes lessons learned and provides practical advice about how and when to use innovation tools. It compares innovation tools with traditional functional tools. It discusses the steps involved in identifying appropriate tools, and provides cautions on the constraints of the various innovation tools and on the challenges of implementation.

Purpose of the Book

Public managers and private managers who interact with government face daunting challenges in this new information and service-oriented economy. Self-regulation makes it difficult for the government to respond quickly to a changing environment. Many public managers remain wedded to the certainty of bureaucratic command and control—it got them to their present position and it has worked more often than it has failed. Nevertheless, we believe that in the future the creative public manager will need to use innovation tools to succeed.

This does not mean that managers do not need budget, personnel, and reporting systems. It does means they will need more than these traditional tools. For example, budget systems may require a performance element. Reporting systems may need to feed into worker analysis of their own work processes.

The purpose of this book is to demonstrate the use of some of the most typical innovation tools. We also provide managers with a framework for absorbing the essential pieces of the new tools that will surely evolve over the next several years. As long as the management consulting industry is able to bill hours, you can be sure that new tools and modifications of old tools will be developed. Many of these techniques are relatively simple, and some are even useful.

Getting past the hype that seems to accompany these new techniques is important. With care they can be incorporated into a manager's tool kit for influencing organizational behavior. To get past the hype, we suggest that managers do as we have done in this book: define the tool, figure out its basic operational steps, and analyze its costs and benefits. In considering new innovation tools, as well as the ones we have discussed here, we hope you will extend our work further by taking one additional step: analyze costs and benefits specifically as they relate to your own organizational setting.

The creative public manager must continue to search for new tools and new approaches. Experiment, take small risks, ask tough questions of your staff and of yourself. It is our hope that this book will, in some small way, help you address the challenges of a changing public sector.

Acknowledgments

A number of people helped us as we thought about, prepared for, researched, and wrote this book, and we wish to thank them. We both thank the three people who were deans of the Columbia University School of International and Public Affairs while we wrote this book: John Ruggie, Douglas Chalmers, and Lisa Anderson. We are grateful for the support they gave us in encouraging us to combine our roles as administrators, consultants, teachers, and researchers. We thank Ron Brand for introducing us to TQM and to the field of management innovation. We also appreciate the incredibly creative, competent, and diligent work of Molly Spencer (M.P.A., 1997), who was the lead research assistant on this book. Other staff who assisted include Neil Amos, Nancy Degnan, Craig Lustig, Barbara Gombach, Jamie Prijatel, and Megan Watkins. We are both deeply grateful to the creative public managers who appear in the case studies: in Indianapolis, Mayor Stephen Goldsmith and his deputy Bill Stephan; in the New York City DPR, Betsy Gotbaum, Ed Norris, Warren DeLuca, William Dalton, Henry Stern, Ian Shapiro, John Ifcher, and Robert Garafola; at America Works, Lee Bowes, Peter Cove, Richard Greenwald, and Phillip Jones. The talent, dedication, and sense of excellence of all of these managers drove them to find better ways of doing business. They represent the type of managers who are transforming our public sector and deserve our admiration.

On a personal note, Steve thanks his wife, Donna Fishman, who is a creative public sector professional with New York City's

Community Service Society and has helped him reality test many of the ideas in this book. He also thanks his daughters, Gabriella Rose and Ariel Mariah, for reminding him of why the future of public management matters. Steve also thanks his parents, Marvin and Shirley, his brother Robby, and his sisters Judith and Myra.

Bill thanks his wife Karen for making the struggle worth it and always pushing him to be better. He also thanks his daughter, Annemarie, for her smiles, her love, and her future. Finally, he remembers his parents for stressing the importance of education.

New York, New York   Steven Cohen
January 1998   William Eimicke

The Authors

Steven Cohen is associate dean of the School of International and Public Affairs and since 1985 has been director of Columbia's Graduate Program in Public Policy and Administration. He received his B.A. degree (1974) in political science from Franklin College of Indiana and his M.A. (1977) and Ph.D. (1979) degrees in political science from the State University of New York at Buffalo. Cohen served as a policy analyst in the U.S. Environmental Protection Agency (EPA) from 1977 to 1978 and from 1980 to 1981, and as a consultant to the EPA from 1981 to 1991. He is author of *The Effective Public Manager* (1988) and coauthor of *Environmental Regulation Through Strategic Planning* (1991), *Total Quality Management in Government* (1993), and *The New Effective Public Manager* (1995).

William Eimicke is director of the School of International and Public Affairs Public Management Training Center and Program in Politics and Public Policy. He received his B.A. degree (1970) in political science, his M.P.A. degree (1971), and his Ph.D. degree (1973), also in political science, from Syracuse University. Eimicke was director of housing for the state of New York from 1985 to 1988; deputy secretary to the governor of New York from 1983 to 1985; deputy commissioner of the New York City Department of Housing, Preservation and Development from 1979 to 1982; and assistant director of the New York City Office of Management and Budget from 1978 to 1979. In 1993 he served on Vice President Al Gore's National Performance Review, which sought to "reinvent" the federal government. He is the author of numerous articles on critical public policy and management issues.

Tools for Innovators

Chapter One

Understanding and Applying Innovation Strategies in the Public Sector

In July 1997, a marvel of scientific and management innovation landed on Mars. The Pathfinder mission was a tremendous success—the result of a series of pathbreaking management innovations brought to the National Aeronautics and Space Administration (NASA) by its administrator, Daniel Goldin. One news account at the time noted: "In the past several years NASA has been quietly reinventing itself. The slow and swollen agency that grew so fat in the post-Apollo years has been painstakingly downsizing itself to something approaching the agency it was first designed to be when it was founded in the late 1950s: a crew of garage engineers cobbling spacecraft from simple parts and getting the job done both on budget and on deadline" (Kluger, 1997, p. 32).

Goldin led a major effort in strategic planning, benchmarking, Total Quality Management (TQM), and reengineering. Under his guidance, NASA totally rethought its standard operating procedures (SOPs) and approach to space travel. Goldin radically revised NASA's organizational culture. The evidence of this transformation can be found by comparing the 1976 Viking Mars missions to the 1997 Pathfinder program—two Viking spacecraft cost $3 billion in 1997 dollars, while two Pathfinder ships cost $500 million, and Pathfinder included the Sojourner rover, a two-foot-long robotic vehicle that conducted a scientific investigation of Mars—and in the fact that Goldin was one of the few senior managers from the Bush administration who held his job into the Clinton administration. Goldin infused NASA with a new sense of strategic purpose. That strategy was reflected in the Mars Pathfinder mission objectives that appeared on NASA's World Wide Web home page in summer 1997. One of these objectives was to make Pathfinder "faster, better, and cheaper," to develop the mission in three years at a cost lower than $150 million dollars, and thus to demonstrate the feasibility of developing a simple, low-cost system at a fixed price.

Goldin's use of a wide variety of management innovation techniques resulted in a new approach to space travel—one that fits within the political and budgetary parameters of the late 1990s. In our view, nothing presents the possibilities of innovation management more graphically than the accomplishments of the Pathfinder program in summer 1997. Can these lessons be applied to management issues on Earth? We think they can.

This book describes strategies for bringing management innovation into public sector organizations and develops ideas about how and when to deploy several specific strategies. We discuss management innovation conceptually and in relation to some specific techniques of management innovation now being tested by creative public sector managers. These techniques include strategic planning, reengineering, TQM, benchmarking, performance measurement, team management, and privatization. This is not an exhaustive list of the myriad of innovation techniques available to managers. Rather, it is a set of the most common innovation techniques now applied in the public sector.

Although we consider each technique separately, in practice they often are implemented in concert. Indeed, these techniques should in no way be seen as mutually exclusive. In fact, one of the major assumptions of this book is that despite consultants' and others' advocacy of one technique or another as the right one to follow, effective management innovation requires blending and tailoring a variety of innovation techniques to suit an organization's unique culture and environment.

The Concept of Public Sector Management Innovation

For us, public sector management innovation is best defined as *the development and implementation of new policy designs and new standard operating procedures by public organizations to address public policy problems.* It is important to emphasize that we are dealing with both the *design* and the *management* of policies and programs. Bureaucracy was created to provide stable, *preformed decisions* (to use the classic formulation of Kaufman, 1960) about specific, relatively stable phenomena and stimuli. These SOPs were designed to be long-standing and unchanging.

As the world enters the twenty-first century, societies and economies are rapidly changing in response to new technologies that have facilitated greater exchange and economic and social interdependency. This accelerated rate of change has challenged the traditional bureaucratic form of organization and thus requires the development of new methods for rapidly modifying organizational strategies and the procedures used to implement those strategies.

Several studies of successful public management innovation illustrate the nature of management change processes in the public sector. Olivia Golden (1990) studied innovation in public sector human service organizations and "the implications of innovation by groping along" (p. 219). She studied the winners of the 1986 Ford Foundation Awards program for innovation in public management and tested the use of two models of innovation in the public sector. The *policy planning model* emphasizes innovation through creative policy design. In this framework, innovation is the task performed by policy analysts, and line bureaucrats oppose innovation as they defend their traditional SOPs. The *groping-along model* emphasizes field-level experimentation with new ideas. According to Golden, "We cannot know ahead of time what the results of our ideas will be, because the complexities of the real world cannot be anticipated and because ideas divorced from rich operational experience are so general that they are likely to be systematically wrong. Because we cannot know the results of our ideas, we need to try them out in action and learn from experience; based on that learning, we may need to modify not only our actions but also the policy idea and the original objectives" (1990, p. 226).

Mary Bryna Sanger and Martin Levin (1992) built on Golden's analysis in their study of more than twenty-five successful public sector innovations. They concluded that public management innovation is rarely characterized by revolutionary breakthroughs. Instead, it typically involves rearranging old practices in new ways.

In organizational learning, rational analysis of options before implementation seems to be less useful than evaluation, and subsequent modification, of programs already under way.

Both of these studies indicate that innovative programs and effective program outcomes seem to be a function of a spirit of experimentation and a willingness to adopt and discard practices rapidly in the face of evidence about the effectiveness of those practices. Although this research does not distinguish the design of organizational routines from the design of programs and policies, we believe that these findings are applicable to both.

The supposed failure of various organizational reform efforts is frequently a result of attempts to apply an organizational reform methodology quickly and uniformly throughout an organization. Rather than understanding these methods as instruments of incremental organizational reform, senior management and their high-priced consultants see these ideas as all-encompassing organizational ideologies. They are oversold and misapplied, and often fail for those reasons.

Successful innovation is often incremental and small scale because the factors that condition the success of innovative practices vary according to the organization's internal capacity, external environment, and goals or mission. Each organization is different and faces varied situations at particular points in time. The techniques required to promote organizational innovation must therefore be determined situationally. Furthermore, the stability of the organization's environment changes over time, requiring varied degrees of innovation. Finally, the internal social structure and the capacity of an organization to support and carry out changed SOPs will also vary. When considering the application of management change techniques, one size does not fit all.

In our own efforts to adapt TQM to specific government situations, we developed a *project-oriented* approach (Cohen and Eimicke, 1994a). This approach represents an explicit recognition that the specific shape that TQM should take varies in each and every work situation. The general principles of TQM could be taught in two or three hours, but the actual application would evolve over time in individual organizational units.

Our TQM work taught us several other things about bringing innovative practices into organizations. First, TQM in isolation was not a sufficient approach to making organizations agile and effective in rapidly changing conditions. If the organization's overall strategy was faulty, or if its basic agencywide systems were in massive disrepair—for example, a personnel system that prevented hiring and retaining quality staff—TQM would have the same effect as rearranging deck chairs on the Titanic. Through TQM, an effective practice for posting jobs or providing promotional opportunities might have been designed, but if no one got hired or promoted because the overall system was flawed, the newly designed processes would have no real impact on the organization's performance. An example of the type of system failure we refer to here might be a hiring process with so many approval steps that excellent candidates attracted through a newly redesigned posting and advertising process would take jobs with other organizations because of delays in getting hired.

Our TQM experiences started us thinking about how and when to utilize other organizational reform strategies:

- Under what conditions is imagination dry and the need to benchmark other organizational practices acute?
- When should the high organizational cost of top-down, large-scale system reengineering be accepted?
- When should an organization substitute a contractor's work for its own?
- When has the organization's environment changed sufficiently to warrant a revision of its mission, focus, and strategy?
- To what degree should team processes replace individual assignments?

These questions encouraged us to develop an overall framework for management innovation strategies that delineates their characteristics as techniques of change and assesses their utility in specific situations.

The Purpose of Management Innovation

The first question that public managers face is, *What aspect of the organization are we trying to change?* The answer to this question can lead to the use of a particular innovation technique or sequence of techniques.

The first step in addressing this question involves identifying the potential arenas of organizational change. In our view there are three arenas, each calling for different organizational change techniques.

1. *External:* The arena that comprises the organization's environment. Issues addressed here include the organization's mission, resource base, market niche, political support and opposition.
2. *Macro-internal:* The arena of organizational behavior dealing with large-scale, organizationwide systems and infrastructure that support the activities of individual organizational units. This includes the organization's budget, purchasing, personnel, information, security, and communication systems, as well as other similar support systems and structures.
3. *Micro-internal:* The arena of organizational behavior that takes place within individual organizational units as SOPs are developed, implemented, and analyzed. It also includes behavioral incentives or motivation and the entire realm of individual and group interpersonal relations at work.

An organization can have needs in all three arenas, and every technique we discuss in subsequent chapters can have some utility in each arena, but different techniques tend to have greater usefulness in particular arenas. For example, strategic planning is the best method for dealing with issues that appear in the external arena, reengineering is well suited for some macro-internal issues, and TQM is an excellent method for addressing issues in the micro-internal arena.

To apply innovation techniques effectively, a shared definition of each technique is needed. This book describes and assesses strategic planning, reengineering, TQM, benchmarking, performance measurement, team management, and privatization. We define these techniques, describe how they work, and discuss the typical benefits or impacts and costs of using them.

A Framework for Analyzing the Use of Management Innovation Tools

The metaphors of tool and craft are essential to understanding the process of bringing change into organizational settings. We begin with the assumption that organizational management and change is a craft, not a science; and we consciously label the innovation techniques *tools*. The effective public manager applies these tools in an iterative process to build solutions to management problems. With experience, the craftsperson notices patterns and tendencies that allow the tools to be deployed more effectively. The millionth time the carpenter places the nail on the wood, he or she knows where and when to strike the nail with maximum effect.

What conditions affect the use of innovation tools? When do we use the saw? When do we take out the drill? When do we need to hammer a nail? When do we need a strategy? When do we need to benchmark? When must we reengineer? At what point might TQM be introduced? The management craftsperson must learn to identify the proper conditions and the likely impact of a specific tool in a particular situation in a given environment.

Organizational change is a modification of the way an organization responds to specific stimuli. It includes the specific changes brought about, as well as the process by which change takes place. In other words, organizational change may result in changed organizational outputs or outcomes, or in an increased capacity to produce new outputs or outcomes. Another possible goal of organizational change is to create a more agile organization.

Managers have at their disposal a broad range of tools that can be used to bring about organizational change. They have *traditional functional tools*, such as budgets, financial control systems, and information systems. They have *human resource management tools*, such as merit reward systems, competitive hiring procedures, and affirmative action. They have *organizational structure tools*, such as reorganization or decentralization. Managers can also use the media, customers, and other external parties to change the behavior of members of the organization. We discussed these traditional tools in detail in *The New Effective Public Manager* (Cohen and Eimicke, 1995).

In addition to these tools, managers also have available the range of innovation tools we discuss in this book: reengineering, TQM, benchmarking, team processes, strategic planning, and privatization. All of these techniques have as their aim influencing the behavior of the people who implement public programs. In the case of privatization and public and private partnerships, public managers may be trying to change the behavior of nongovernmental players. But public managers typically focus their change

efforts on government employees. As they progress through the
work of innovative change, it is essential to bear in mind the
dependent variable in this relationship: the behavior of public
implementors.

The Tools

The first factor that the management innovator must consider is
the nature of the tool itself: What does the technique do? What
kind of organizational learning does it facilitate? How much does
it cost to do? Many innovation techniques require investment in
teachers or consultants. Most require investment of staff time.
Some require investment in computers or communication equipment. Benchmarking frequently involves travel costs. Privatization
requires substantial transaction costs if contracts are let and mon-
itored. It is wise to project the potential costs and benefits of
deploying a tool before it is utilized.

The six chapters in Part One of this book provide operational
definitions of these innovation tools. Each tool has proponents
who would like people to believe that their favorite tool is the management silver bullet. We have found that each of these tools has
value, but none is a cure-all. Sometimes a reengineered solution
will be a disaster, destroying a functioning system within an organization and replacing it with a nonfunctioning system. At times,
political conditions do not allow a government organization to
engage in benchmarking. Similarly, employing TQM in an organization that has not developed a coherent strategy can result in
people doing the wrong thing more effectively.

The first job of the innovator is to learn about the inherent
strengths and weaknesses of the tool that derive from the tool's definition. With that understanding in place, the organizational innovator must ask some questions about the organization itself and
about its environment.

The Organization

Organizations are complex social systems built on patterns of
human interaction developed over time in the performance of
tasks. An innovator must learn about the organization's culture:

How are things done around here? What is the informal organization? Who makes things happen? What types of change have been successfully brought about here in the past? What types of change have failed? By studying the development and demise of SOPs in specific organizations, a manager can learn about the organization's patterns and capabilities. This can help the manager to develop a feel for which tool is most appropriate for the specific changes being sought.

We deliberately use the word *feel* in this context. We are convinced that a large number of complex, interconnected variables must be understood in order to determine appropriate change strategies. Tools must be applied gently to test their effect before their use is attempted throughout an organization. In some cases the tool should never be used in certain parts of the organization.

One of the reasons that much real change is gradual, incremental, and "organic" is that its success often depends on the manager's in-depth understanding and intuitive craftlike feel for the vagaries of the organization's life. An effective change agent must either have this knowledge from personal experience or be skilled at drawing it out of others. In any event, attempting to innovate without deep organizational knowledge is like trying to repair a delicate stopwatch with a sledgehammer. Any change that occurs without an understanding of the internal social system of the organization should be treated as a lucky guess and nothing more.

The Environment

Public organizations operate in a media fishbowl and must function in a manner circumscribed by laws and regulations. Laws authorize, shape, and constrain the actions of public organizations. The ability to respond to external stimuli is modified by the political process that creates these rules. Therefore, the use of innovation tools within an organization must be sensitive to the rules governing an organization's behavior. You might find a great program idea by benchmarking an organization in another jurisdiction, and then learn that the practice is illegal in your state.

The organization's strategy is the tool most dependent on an accurate reading of the organization's environment. The goals of a public organization must be designed to elicit both political support and resources from the organization's environment. An effective strategist must understand the politics and the array of social and economic forces related to the organization's work. He or she must be able to project the likely impact of changes in the organization's goals, programs, and activities on its customers, enemies, and friends.

The organization's environment also affects the views and behaviors of those within the organization. If the economy is bad and budgets are being cut, the members of the organization may react by being scared, defensive, and resistant to change. Or they may embrace change as a survival strategy, recognizing that their best defense in a cutback environment is enhanced productivity. They may even offer to take on additional functions as a way of enhancing job security.

Management experts with a private sector orientation often see political factors as illegitimate, exogenous factors in the process of organizational change. In our view, in the case of public organizations such political factors should be conceptualized as central determinants of the ultimate parameters of organizational change. Politics sets the boundaries for what is feasible in the public sector. To ignore that is to disregard the public in *public sector.*

The Risks

The preceding pages contain what largely is an argument for craftlike care in the process of changing an organization's mission, processes, and capacities. Now we need to turn that argument on its head a bit, because no matter how careful a manager is, change inherently implies some element of risk. In our view, a changing environment makes stable, unchanging, bureaucratic procedures risky as well, but at least this risk is the risk of a known quantity. The external environment is changing, but dealing with it in a fixed manner—that is, according to established, bureaucratic procedures—enables you to measure your declining effectiveness in precise ways. This is not an approach that has much to recommend it.

To bring about change in an organization a manager must be willing to gamble. The change you are hoping to bring about might not work. If you are careful, the setback will not be catastrophic. We generally suggest small steps and hedging your bets.

When using an innovation tool, plan for its possible failure as well as for its possible success. Be ready with a plan B if plan A fails. Being willing to try something new need not require recklessness.

Top managers must be willing to take risks and to tolerate risk taking among middle management and staff. That means that well-conceived experiments that fail must be rewarded from time to time, and whenever possible, not punished.

Applications of the Innovation Framework

This book provides the reader with specific definitions and analysis of the costs and benefits of the innovation tools it introduces. In addition, it provides operational definitions of the tools and each chapter includes a section about how the tool works. We suggest step-by-step instructions for applying the tool once you have decided to do so. This approach serves to familiarize you with a full and objective description of the innovation tool, thus giving you the information you need to decide whether to utilize the tool in your own organization. Because most of the books on these tools are written by advocates, an advantage of this book is that we are not biased toward any particular tool.

Our approach to these techniques as tools rather than as all-encompassing answers is designed to encourage you to develop your own analysis of where and when to apply each tool. You will need to decide whether to apply several tools in combination or in a particular sequence as part of an overall effort to bring new ways of thinking and operating into your organization.

Unfortunately we cannot sit within your organization and provide you with an understanding of its social structure and environment. That is an analytic and intuitive process you must conduct for yourself. However, we can tell you some stories or cases from organizations that have attempted to innovate. The chapters in Part Two include an example from government (the case of New York City's Department of Parks and Recreation, told in Chapter Eight); an example of a public-private partnership including a government, a nonprofit organization, and private players (the case of Indianapolis and its Private Industry Council, presented in Chapter Nine); and a case of a private company that performs a privatized public function (America Works Inc., a firm that helps welfare recipients find employment, discussed in Chapter Ten). Each of these case studies presents information about the organization's environment and internal functioning. The innovation tools attempted and the results of those attempts are described. Although examining case studies cannot substitute for trying these tools yourself, it can provide a map of the path followed by other innovators.

Organizational change is not an easy process. There are no shortcuts, technological fixes, or magic bullets. You end up doing a lot of slogging through the mud because in the end you are trying to influence the behavior of people. Many people resist change because they are comfortable with how things are: "If it's not broken, why fix it?"

The contemporary world is characterized by rapid changes in technology, society, politics, communications, and culture. The pace of change is accelerating and effective organizations have little choice but to keep up. The remainder of this book provides insights and lessons drawn from some experiences that were not always pleasant. We hope you find them helpful.

Part One

Public Sector Innovation Tools

| Strategic Planning

In *Strategic Planning for Public Managers,* James Mercer observed that "at least three decades ago, Peter Drucker defined planning as actions taken right now to reach tomorrow's objectives. His definition still holds; planning means deciding what has to be done to prepare a given organization for the future" (1991, p. 17). C. W. Hofer and D. E. Schendel (1978) define strategy as the basic pattern of current and planned resource deployments and environmental interactions that indicate how the organization will achieve its objectives. Strategic planning's oldest roots are in military decision-making processes. "In the context of military decision-making, the concept implies a comprehensive preparedness sufficient to meet any and all eventualities" (Sutherland, 1978, p. 427). This notion of comprehensive protection and anticipation is central to strategic planning.

Strategic planning in the public sector is a process that enables an organization and its leaders to make resource allocation and related service output decisions that emphasize the organization's mission (King and Cleland, 1978). In *The New Effective Public Manager* (Cohen and Eimicke, 1995, p. 196), we observed that "a strategy attempts to delineate the resources that will be used to pay for specific activities designed to accomplish specific objectives. Strategy formulation begins with the identification of objectives and the determination of methods for reaching objectives. These objectives and activities are then scaled to fit within resource constraints. Each element of a strategy (objectives, activities and resources) is constrained by political, social, economic and environmental variables. The objectives and activities of public organizations are constrained by the formal authority provided by statute."

An alternate view of strategic planning is offered by John Bryson and William Roering (1996). They define strategic planning as "a set of concepts, procedures, and tools designed to help leaders, managers, and public administrators figure out what their communities and organizations should do to survive and prosper" (p. 479). Although this definition begins to describe strategic planning, it does not include strategic planning's orientation toward rational resource allocation.

As Bernard Taylor noted in the *Strategic Planning and Management Handbook* (King and Cleland, 1987), one of the primary forces in the evolution of strategic planning is the necessity of managers having better control over resources (Taylor, 1987). Although its modern roots took hold in the development of long-range planning in the 1950s and 1960s, strategic planning gained particular popularity in the 1970s when the relative wealth of the postwar era had dissipated and both public and private resources were more constrained than before (Makridakis and Héau, 1987). Most scholars agree that although strategic planning may help managers to figure out what their organizations should do to survive and prosper, its greatest value is in helping align an organization's mission, goals, and means for achieving them with its available resources.

How Strategic Planning Works

In the public sector, the manager's concern about resource constraints is compounded by political, social, economic, and other environmental factors as well as by the organization's public mandate. Given the number of variables a public manager must consider while fulfilling the role of leader in an organization, the comprehensive nature of strategic planning makes it a particularly important tool.

A strategic planning exercise typically involves an organizationwide initiative to reformulate goals and develop new methods of achieving those goals. At a minimum, managers from key organizational units are involved in the process. Sometimes participation is broader, involving staff from throughout the organization. Some organizations also include key stakeholders in their strategic planning processes. Bryson (1995, p. 27) defines a stakeholder as "any person, group, or organization that can place a claim on an organization's attention, resources, or output, or is affected by that output."

Although not every organization undertakes strategic planning in exactly the same manner, any strategic planning process involves the same basic elements. First, an organization must commit to the strategic planning process and prepare itself to begin the process. Subsequent stages include developing or refining the organization's mission, or both; scanning the organization's external and internal environments; assessing organizational strengths and weaknesses; developing concrete strategies by which to achieve the organization's mission; and developing a plan for evaluation (Mercer, 1991).

As strategic planning begins, new information about the impact of the organization's environment on the organization's goals and activities is presented and assessed. Meetings are held to stimulate the creation of new approaches to the organization's mission and work. An inventory of the organization's capabilities and needs is also conducted to determine its capacity to implement the new strategy.

In an earlier work (Cohen and Kamieniecki, 1991), Cohen described a strategic planning process that took place in the U.S. Environmental Protection Agency's (EPA) Office of Underground Storage Tanks. The outline presented in Exhibit 2.1 is based on that strategy development process and is drawn from that analysis. Strategy development is a form of rational decision making. It is an effort to develop objectives and to devise a number of alternative methods for achieving those objectives.

In our view, the purpose of strategy development is not to build a rigid plan that must be followed. The world changes too rapidly and the information requirements of a true master plan are not feasible in the real world. A strategy is an alternative to responding merely to the issue or stimuli of the moment. The aim should be to develop a general map that identifies the place to which you would like to go and the impediments and opportunities that will hinder or facilitate your organization's ability to reach that place.

Exhibit 2.1. The Steps of Strategic Planning.

I.   Problem and opportunity analysis.

   A. The mission statement.

      1. What programs and services should we be providing?

      2. Why do we exist?

      3. How are we unique?

      4. Who are our customers/users?

      5. What are the three to five most important programs we provide now and that we will provide in the future?

      6. What do we do best now and what will we do best in the future?

      7. How are we different from the way we were three to five years ago?

      8. How are we most likely to be different three to five years from now?

      9. What are our major outputs and outcomes and how can we measure them?

   B. Environmental scanning: the identification of future challenges and opportunities.

      1. What is the source of the challenges/threats and opportunities to our organization?

      2. Why do these challenges and opportunities exist?

II. Identification and analysis of players.

   A. Who is creating problems, challenges, and opportunities for our organization?

      1. What internal groups or parties are involved?

      2. What is their perspective?

      3. How will these parties affect our mission?

      4. What external groups or parties are involved?

      5. What is their perspective?

      6. How will these parties affect our mission?

Exhibit 2.1. *(continued)*

III. Historical analysis.

A. What created these problems and opportunities, and how did we get here?

B. How have different levels of our organization and the individuals within the organization responded to key challenges and opportunities in the past?

C. How long have these challenges and opportunities existed?

D. What attempts have been made at preventing problems and at exploiting opportunities? (Search for analogous situations.)

E. How successful/unsuccessful were these attempts?

F. How have the parties involved responded to these efforts?

IV. Organizational and situational analysis.

A. Organizational strengths, weaknesses, accomplishments, opportunities, and threats.

1. What are our organization's strengths and weaknesses?

2. What opportunities and threats do we face in our current environment?

3. What are our organization's goals?

V. Strategy formulation.

A. Defining and accomplishing success: short-term objectives and tasks.

B. Defining and accomplishing success: long-term objectives and tasks.

VI. Preimplementation projection.

A. Measure fit and feasibility.

VII. Evaluation and midcourse correction.

A. Make incremental adjustments to programs and policies.

B. Collect data on routine performance.

C. Conduct periodic formal evaluation and correction.

Source: Cohen and Kamieniecki, copyright © 1991 by Westview Press. Reprinted by permission of Westview Press.

As Exhibit 2.1 indicates, a strategy consists of seven general elements:

1. Problem and opportunity analysis
2. Identification and analysis of players
3. Historical analysis
4. Organizational and situational analysis
5. Concrete strategy formulation
6. Preimplementation projection
7. Evaluation and midcourse correction

We prefer this seven-step approach to strategic planning and have seen it work well for both public and private organizations, large and small.

Problem and Opportunity Analysis

The first stage of strategic planning is sometimes termed environmental scanning (Mercer, 1991). It involves analysis of the factors in an organization's environment that influence and shape the organization's mission and character. An environmental scan helps the strategic planning team to view the organization's current position "in light of past events, current conditions, and future possibilities" (Mercer, 1991, p. 39). This activity allows the organization to identify issues and trends—both opportunities and constraints—that are essential to its future (Mercer, 1991). Such an analysis is an essential first step in ensuring that the organization's members have a shared sense of purpose. This scan provides information on the set of possible organizational conditions and missions.

The organization's central mission must be drawn from the set of feasible options. On the basis of that mission the organization must develop its sense of shared purpose. Such a sense of purpose is important in eliciting coordinated and consistent behaviors from the members of the organization. As Bryson and Roering (1996) note, strategic planning efforts that are highly comprehensive and rational will fail without a clear sense of organizational purpose. The plan cannot simply be the shortest distance between two points; rather, it must be a path that elicits and heightens support from its organization.

One method among many that could be used to operationalize this analysis of an organization's environment is to develop a
mission statement. To ensure that the mission statement is not a
static document, we typically recommend that an organization project future challenges and opportunities that may affect its mission.
Exhibit 2.1 includes a list of questions that might be addressed
in developing a mission statement. These questions utilize a variety of approaches to determine what the organization is about,
what it does, for whom it does it, what it is good at, what it produces, what the impact of its outputs is, how this has changed in
the past, and how it may change in the future. In our experience,
these questions often result in sharply diverging responses from
members of an organization. Often the organization's members
have different cognitive maps of the organization's products and
mission. In the Environmental Protection Agency, for example,
some saw the organization's mission as preventing all pollution.
Others saw it as reducing pollution, whereas a third group saw the
mission as getting people out of harm's way and promoting public
health. A number of people held that the mission included all of
these elements.

Even organizations with relatively straightforward programs,
such as parks and sanitation departments, often have unclear missions, or at a minimum, confused priorities. This divergence may
increase if stakeholders are involved in the process. The difficulty
then becomes creating criteria for judging the competing claims
of all players (Bryson and Roering, 1996). William King and David
Cleland (1978, pp. 142, 143) note that "the primary mistakes that
have been made by organizations in their selection of a mission
have been treating their basic purpose as being obvious or prede-
termined." In fact, organizations have choices in selecting a mission, and even if they do not see it that way, some interest group
probably will.

Another key aspect of the environmental scan is the issue of
attracting resources. In developing a strategy, an organization
should address one central question: *What can we do that will attract
resources?* Strategy is about setting priorities and defining, developing, and defending organizational capacities that society values
enough to pay for. In the private sector, an organization's success
is measured by its profit, market share, and return on equity. In

the public and nonprofit sectors, success is measured by political support, media image, tangible accomplishments, and ultimately, budget. Mercer (1991) ties the success of any strategic planning system to the organization's budget and its budgeting processes. He believes that "a strategic planning process unrelated to the budget is without substance," and that any successful strategic planning process must link "comprehensive planning and the annual operating and capital budgets" (p. 7). Therefore, assessing the environment to determine an organization's mission should not be an abstract analysis of what the organization would like to accomplish as an organization. Instead, it should be a hardheaded analysis of which mission will elicit support and ultimately resources.

An organization cannot simply reinvent itself by identifying a more attractive mission. The parameters of an organization's mission are established by its history, customers, image, and existing capability. In the public sector, mission is also constrained by the organization's legal authority and by other formal delineations of its charge. In some cases public organizations have missions that make it difficult to generate political support and resources. For example, people may support more resources for prisons but resist funding for rehabilitating criminals. It may be clear to professionals that rehabilitation is desirable, but a prison system may find it politically expedient to focus its mission and image on punishment.

The process of developing an organization's mission requires leadership but should also involve organized staff participation and an effort to develop a consensus. For a mission to be effectively translated into organizational behavior, it must represent a set of values shared by most of the people within the organization. Once a mission is identified, it is important that it be communicated and reinforced on a regular basis. This communication and reinforcement begins with formal communiqués, retreats, and meetings. Ultimately the organization's reward system must be modified to communicate and reinforce mission.

The next step in analyzing an organization's problems and opportunities is to project the organization's mission into the future and identify potential threats and opportunities. In the Harvard Policy Model of strategic planning, this is referred to as SWOT (strengths, weaknesses, opportunities, threats) analysis (Bryson and

Roering, 1996). Ideally, an assessment of an organization's strengths and weaknesses will have been undertaken during the mission development process. Projecting these strengths and weaknesses into the future to identify potential threats and opportunities is the next step.

A number of questions should be addressed in analyzing threats and opportunities. Most of these questions relate to changes in the organization's environment and attempts to project the impact of those changes on the organization's work, outputs, and outcomes. Key questions address how trends in demographics, technology, culture, social values and needs, economic development, wealth and perceived economic needs, and political views, support, and coalitions might affect the organization and its mission:

- How will a changing world affect our organization?
- Will demands for our services increase or decrease?
- Will we be asked to take on new or modified missions?
- How will the problems we are seeking to address be perceived by the mass public and by various elites?
- What types of resource demands and organizational stress should we anticipate and attempt to address?

Identification and Analysis of Players

Once the environment has been scanned for threats and opportunities, the next part of strategy development is to identify and analyze the people and groups that interact with the organization. In some government settings this particular task must be pursued with care to avoid the impression that you are creating a list of friends and enemies. In many cases this analysis will be conducted informally and will not be included in a formal strategy statement.

It is extremely important to understand the players in your organization's environment as well as their motivation. What type of pressures are influencing their behavior? This analysis can also help the organization to refine its mission further, because if the list of players is comprehensive, it should "encompass all of those who have a claim on the organization, and thereby reflect all that the organization is about and all that it should be seeking." In this way the analysis of key players can act as a "checklist for managers to use in testing and evaluating proposed objectives or actions" (King and Cleland, 1978, pp. 156, 152). Here again a major issue is the definition of criteria by which to prioritize the importance to the organization of each person's or group's concerns.

Historical Analysis

To know where an organization is, we need to know where it has been. In a public sector governed by politicians with relatively short time horizons, organizations often willfully develop amnesia. The same mistakes are made again and again, and institutional memory is sometimes derided as "old thinking" and the mistakes of our predecessors.

A key element of historical analysis is to identify past patterns of cause and effect. What factors led to past success and failure? In what way did the organization's actions lead to specific successes and failures? To what extent were these successes and failures caused by events external to the organization? Could these external parties have been influenced or was the result inevitable?

Another important step is the search for analogous situations. In the Superfund toxic waste cleanup program of the 1980s, the EPA built on the lessons learned in the sewage treatment construction grants program of the 1970s. Because many parts of the Superfund program required large-scale construction to contain and clean up waste, the EPA looked to its other major construction grants program when searching for an analogous model. In the mid-1980s, when the EPA began to create a program to clean up leaking underground storage tanks, it sought to learn from similar activities in the Superfund program. It is true that analogies can be false and there is always a danger that the EPA may have tried too hard to imitate its earlier programs directly. However, unless an organization understands its own history, it is unlikely to search for analogies and learn from the past.

Organizational and Situational Analysis

The next step in strategy development is analysis of the organization's current capabilities and current opportunities and threats. Three key questions must be addressed: (1) What are we capable of doing? (2) What is expected of us? and (3) What environmental factors will impede or facilitate our work? This step involves revisiting the environmental scan with an eye to how various environmental factors influence the organization's daily operations and capacity.

The organizational analysis requires a realistic assessment of the organization's accomplishments and distinctive competencies. Strategic objectives must not be set in a vacuum. They must fit within the parameters of organizational capability. While organizations can develop new capacities and purchase capacities they do not have, organizational learning and contracting out take time and still require management capacity. Each organizational direction pursued forecloses other directions. These opportunity costs must always be assessed when pursuing a new organizational mission, or when determining a set of new objectives in pursuit of an existing mission.

The best way to appraise organizational capacity is to inventory accomplishments. Actions do speak louder than words. People within an organization may believe that the organization possesses a particular capability, and management may share that perception, but perception is not always reality. People may occupy a piece of organizational turf but not actually do the work for which they claim credit. An organization may have a number of people with skills and credentials on paper, but those skills may have grown dormant. For these reasons, the best way to assess an organization's capacity is to describe and assess its outputs.

The situational analysis attempts to place the organization and its capabilities within the context of its environment. Now that we know what we do around here, who values our work? What resources can this work attract? What changes do we need to make to maintain or enhance our current position? Can our organization actually make those changes, and if so, what price would we pay?

This effort to scan the organization's environment is a crucial element of strategy formulation. It is necessary to begin strategic planning by assessing an organization's mission (as discussed in the first step), and it must be done again when a strategist is developing operational objectives. Assessing mission requires that a manager develop and interact with a network of key informants among interest groups, elected leaders and their staffs, and other opinion leaders. The manager must "take the temperature" of these key players and attempt to elicit reactions to potential scenarios that the organization might pursue.

The result of this assessment is the identification of operational objectives. These objectives are built on a solid understanding of the organization's capabilities and environment. Once these capabilities are determined, the strategist is ready to detail the organization's operational or concrete strategy. After the objectives are developed, they must be linked to the resources that will be devoted to achieving them (King and Cleland, 1978).

Concrete Strategy Formulation

The next step in strategy formulation is to identify the specific short-term and long-term steps involved in accomplishing the organization's objectives. Mercer (1991, p. 73) defines strategies as "the specific directional actions that define how the organizational mission is to be achieved." The best short-term strategy is essentially a work plan. It identifies the organization's immediate goals and provides details on who will do what to achieve those goals. This includes assignment of tasks to specific organizational units. It also includes operational measures of success.

Sutherland's *Management Handbook for Public Administrators* (1978) suggests that the work plan should address means (How is the objective to be accomplished?), locus (Where is it to be accomplished?), priorities (What is to be accomplished first, given resource constraints?), and standards for evaluation and control. While these tasks and success measures will tend to evolve over the life of the plan, they provide a rough guidepost for implementation.

Preimplementation Projection

Once you have formulated your strategies, you should evaluate their fit and feasibility. For each of your goals, it is important to consider your measures and probabilities of success. Addressing these issues before you begin implementing your plan will help prevent problems and ensure that you make the right decisions.

There are, of course, real limits on the usefulness of these projections, because none of us can predict the future. We consider a projection exercise useful as a way of honing a strategic plan and beginning the process of thinking about potential impacts. However, this particular step should not be allowed to consume very much time or too many resources.

Evaluation and Midcourse Correction

For strategy to be meaningful, it must inject a new thought process into the daily routine of the organization. Once a plan is developed, it must be constantly and rapidly adjusted in the light of experience. Recall that strategic planning evolved as a management tool precisely because the predictions and forecasts made by its antecedent, long-range planning, often failed to occur (Makridakis and Héau, 1987). The comprehensive nature of a strategic plan allows the organization to make adjustments in its operations as the environment changes, or fails to change as management had anticipated it would.

These incremental adjustments must be routine activity, punctuated by occasional efforts to rethink the entire plan. Every once in a while, the organization should step back from its plan to reconnect with fundamentals and reexamine the strategy's underlying premises. The temptation in many organizations is to go on a retreat, or to go through a strategic planning exercise, develop the strategy, and then ignore it. Obviously that sequence of events is a waste of people's time and the organization's resources and ought to be avoided. Key to evaluating a strategy is collecting data on the organization's performance—its processes and outputs. In addition, information on the impact of these outputs should also be collected and analyzed.

Benefits of Strategic Planning

Strategic planning gives an organization a chance to look at itself comprehensively, in the light of new information. When a strategy is developed by a new management team, it provides that team with an opportunity to form a cohesive identity. When it is developed independently by a chief executive, it provides that executive with a medium to define and express his or her leadership. When a strategy is developed with broader participation, it can be used to create a sense of shared mission and values, and as a political tool to develop support for organizational change. In the public sector, an organizational strategy can prevent an agency from being taken in rapidly shifting directions by the political mantra of the moment.

A strategy can help an organization make explicit the trade-offs that are incurred through the decisions they make. Remember that organizational structure is used to break down complex tasks into manageable pieces. When a unit focuses on only a piece of a task, they may develop a process orientation that makes it difficult to judge the impact and implications of their work. A strategic planning process can help correct that tendency by asking organizational units to think about the organization's objectives, outputs, and impacts. It asks people to connect ends to means, a task that often is ignored in many public organizations and large private organizations.

According to Henry Mintzberg (1994, p. 62), "The label for all this effort . . . was planning, but the intention was really control." Mintzberg uses control with a negative connotation and believes that managers undertake strategic planning not for the benefit of the organization but to have control over every aspect of it. It is true that strategic planning has in some cases been used as an instrument of organizational control. We think this is inappropriate. Managers should instead undertake strategic planning according to its best use—to help the organization think.

Costs of Strategic Planning

A high-quality strategic planning process requires significant expenditures of management time and analytic resources. If the analysis is not done well, the organization may misread its environment or misjudge its capabilities. Although organizational change tends to be incremental, some strategic planning exercises assume that organizations are capable of massive, rapid change.

In the public sector, an organizational strategy can create political difficulties because it not only indicates what an organization is planning to do, but it also requires explicit trade-off decisions about what an organization will not do. This statement can stimulate political opposition to the organization, and stimulate publics and interest groups that previously were unaware of the organization's plans.

Although it is never easy to judge the usefulness of a strategic plan, we believe that strategic planning results in organizations that have a clear idea of where they have been, what they are capable of, and where they are going, and that have a rational plan for how to get there.

Chapter Three

Reengineering

Reengineering became a popular management innovation strategy during the mid-1990s. The concept of reengineering was popularized in *Reengineering the Corporation: A Manifesto for Business Revolution* (Hammer and Champy, 1994). Management expert Peter Drucker proclaimed on the book's jacket, "Reengineering is new and it has to be done." But the reengineering revolution actually began in 1990, with the publication of Michael Hammer's original call to arms, "Reengineering Work: Don't Automate, Obliterate" (1990). Hammer argued that despite a decade of restructuring and downsizing, many U.S. corporations were still not meeting their performance goals. The real problem was their outmoded structures and processes, geared toward efficiency and control instead of today's goals of speed, service, and quality.

What should be done? Reengineers argue that it is time to "stop paving over cow paths," to "obliterate them," and to "start over" (Hammer, 1990, p. 104). We need to reject the old and embrace the new, with an expectation of dramatic improvements in performance. In its original construct, reengineering could not be planned meticulously, and it was "an all or nothing proposition with uncertain results" (Hammer, 1990, p. 104).

Reengineering also calls for a cross-functional perspective, which can be achieved only by putting together a team of individuals representing all of the functional units involved in the process to be reengineered. The objective is not to improve the current process, but rather to search for "value-added" changes and new ways to achieve the desired result. Information technology should be used not to automate an existing process but to enable a new one.

The original concept of reengineering was based on seven principles:

1. Organize around outcomes, not tasks.
2. Have those who use the output perform the process.
3. Subsume information processing into real work.
4. Treat geographically dispersed resources as centralized (through information technology).
5. Link parallel activities.
6. Move decisions to the point of work and build control into the process.
7. Capture information only once at the source.

Reengineering also emphasizes the importance of "thinking big," and the need to sustain the drive for dramatic improvement through strong executive leadership.

At its heart reengineering asks, If we were beginning our organization all over again today, how would we structure it for optimum performance? According to Hammer and Champy (1994, p. 31), reengineering is "the fundamental rethinking and radical redesign of business processes to achieve dramatic improvements in contemporary measures of performance, such as cost, quality, service and speed." The four key words in this formal definition are

1. *Fundamental.* What must we accomplish and how can we best accomplish it, ignoring what is and focusing on what should be?

2. *Radical.* Reengineering is about organizational reinvention—totally disregarding existing structures and processes and initiating completely different ways of getting work done.

3. *Dramatic.* Reengineering is antithetical to incrementalism and continuous improvement. It is the equal of zero-based budgeting for management. Reengineering is for organizations in deep trouble, for those who see big trouble ahead, and for industry leaders seeking cutting-edge methods. It is not about benchmarking or even leapfrogging. It is about extraordinary breakthroughs in performance.

4. *Processes.* Those who are committed to reengineering must abandon familiar notions of task-based thinking and move toward conceptualizing their organizations as a collection of activities that

convert inputs into outputs valued by their customers. The emphasis is on processes, yet reengineering advocates have great difficulty articulating the full meaning and operational characteristics of a process-centered management approach.

To explain what reengineering is, it is helpful to specify what reengineering is not. First, reengineering is not automation—doing the wrong thing more efficiently does not get an organization anywhere. Information technology is an important tool of reengineers, but only as a device that facilitates process redesign.

Second, reengineering is not restructuring or downsizing. It is not about lowering capacity to match lower demand but about doing more with less. And the problem is not in the organization's structure but in the work processes themselves. According to reengineering's proponents, reengineering processes enable an organization to manage without bureaucracy, although how this occurs is not usually explained.

Third, reengineering is not Total Quality Management (TQM). The two methods share a focus on how work is actually accomplished (processes) and a team-based approach to problem solving. TQM, however, emphasizes continuous, incremental improvement while reengineering seeks breakthroughs and dramatic gains by rejecting what is and replacing it with entirely new processes. As the reengineering movement matures, it seems to be evolving away from this dichotomy and embracing continuous improvement as a critical link between radical reengineering interventions.

Finally, reengineering is not a fad and not "more of the same." It is probably too soon to reach a conclusion regarding the characterization of reengineering as a fad, but if it is just a fad, at this time it is at least a long-lasting, widespread, and well-funded one. Studies by independent accounting firms found that by the mid-1990s more than 75 percent of large U.S. corporations had at least experimented with reengineering, spending more than $7 billion on consulting fees in the year studied, and more than $30 billion if the investments in technological upgrading are counted. Hammer (1996) himself reports having trained more than ten thousand people in more than a thousand companies. Reengineering articles number in the hundreds, and media references are in the thousands and increasing daily.

As for the "more of the same" characterization, it certainly is not. Reengineering shares many techniques with other innovation methods, including the use of strategic plans, teams, benchmarking, outsourcing (privatization), and even continuous improvement. Nevertheless, the introduction of the clean-sheet approach and the separation of work processes from organizational structure clearly represented a break from the conventional wisdom. How reengineering has been used and misused in practice is another issue.

An interesting comment on the "more of the same" issue is that a careful review of the four reengineering books written by Champy (1996), Hammer (1990, 1996), or both (Hammer and Champy, 1994) reveals not a single footnote or a bibliography. Even a look through the index of each of the four books reveals little integration of reengineering theory with what came before or with other contemporary management techniques. Peter Drucker is not even listed in the index of the original manifesto (Hammer and Champy, 1994), despite the promotional quote from him on the book's jacket. Pareto does get one notation and Adam Smith several, but if you are convinced that reengineering is more of the same, you will have to find the references without the help of the authors' citations.

In Hammer's more recent work (1996) he has concluded that his original focus on radical, clean-sheet, zero-based management was slightly misplaced. While he notes that managers in the field confirm that this emphasis on the radical is what caught the attention and fancy of practitioners, the process orientation is really what holds the most potential organizational improvement. Hammer now sees that what limited organizations prior to reengineering was being trapped in the industrial revolution's focus on perfecting specialized tasks.

Without reengineering, organizations are doomed to a focus on task improvement when their real problems (and opportunities for improvement) are in their organizationwide processes. Why this is so or how it came to be is not made clear. What needs to be done is to turn the organization ninety degrees on its side and to force management to view the organization laterally instead of vertically. Everything must be rethought and reinvented—work, job titles, job requirements, pay, career paths, performance measurement, management's role, and strategy (Hammer, 1996, pp. xii–xiii). There is a new emphasis on the importance of people, their new roles, and how personnel policies and reward structures must be radically changed if the reengineered organization is to reap the benefits and maintain the gains of its revamped processes. In fact, there is at least as much emphasis on the human relations aspects of the innovation as there is on the work processes.

Reengineering was developed for the private sector, particularly large, geographically dispersed, high-volume U.S. corporations. Is reengineering suitable for government organizations? Although Hammer's original writings make no reference to the public sector, the paperback edition of the original manifesto incorporates questions that the authors are commonly asked, one of which concerns the applicability of reengineering to government. The authors' response is "Without a doubt" (Hammer and Champy, 1994, p. 221).

It is more difficult to apply reengineering to government organizations because they do not have a bottom-line profit. Without that simple measure of overall performance it is difficult to assess the trade-offs between service enhancements and cost reductions. The other major obstacle for reengineering in government is that breaking down departmental barriers within one corporation is far easier than doing it among governmental agencies.

Government agency heads usually have strong ties to the elected chief executive of their jurisdiction and they might even have their own power base and public constituency. In our experience, successful reengineering projects in the public sector usually result in the creation of an entirely new agency. Such dramatic action is necessary to break down the possible resistance of public employee unions and to shift the organizational balance of power from entrenched middle managers with civil service protection to politically accountable appointed commissioners and program directors. The desire of Indianapolis's mayor, Stephen Goldsmith, to "blow-up the welfare department" in order to implement a work-based, performance-driven antipoverty initiative is a good example of a public sector version of reengineering (Schuckel, 1996, p. B7).

We are optimistic about the prospects for reengineering as a productive tool for government innovators. Significant evidence that the technique can work well in government is provided by the National Academy of Public Administration's (NAPA) 1994 report on forty-four successful public agency reengineering efforts during 1993 and 1994. NAPA defines reengineering for the public sector somewhat differently, and this alternative definition is helpful in assessing how success in the public sector might be measured. According to the NAPA report, "Government business process reengineering is a radical improvement approach that critically examines, rethinks and redesigns mission, product and service processes within a political environment. It achieves dramatic mission performance gains from multiple customer and stakeholder perspectives. It is a key part of a process management approach for optimal performance that continually evaluates, adjusts or removes processes" (p. 7).

The NAPA definition makes several key distinctions between private and public reengineering. First, there is the significant impact of the political environment. Second, there is the common circumstance in government of multiple customers, consumers, and stakeholders with different interests and measures of performance. And third, continuous improvement or TQM is often coincident with reengineering in the public sector, while in the private sector they are sometimes seen to be in conflict.

As we review the evolving state of reengineering, it seems clear that there is a growing consensus on the basic nature and components of the strategy, and a diversification in applications, as innovators tailor the methodology to fit the contours of their particular organization. While the shorthand definition, "starting over," is useful, we find that "zero-based budgeting for management" gives a better word picture of reengineering's likely impact on an organization. Zero-based budgeting for management means a clean-sheet analysis of policies, priorities, processes, and resource allocations. It means thinking of one's organization as if it were the first day of one's incorporation or taking of power.

Use of the zero-based budgeting parallel also makes clear that there are direct financial consequences of reengineering: it costs a good deal of time, money, effort, goodwill, processing time, and perhaps even employees to initiate the process, and even its architects predict a 50 to 70 percent failure rate. It involves trade-offs— political, operational, and programmatic. In the public sector, successful reengineering also requires a greater buy-in and a broader consensus than in a private or nonprofit organization.

How Reengineering Works

Most of the initial writings on reengineering are filled with stories and examples of what not to do, but there is very little guidance about what to do. There is nothing resembling an operator's manual or a step-by-step how-to guide.

Early efforts to reengineer in the private sector usually began with four key questions: (1) What is the purpose of this business or agency? (2) What kind of culture do we want? (3) How do we do our work? and (4) With what kind of people do we want to work?

What Is the Purpose of This Business or Agency?

The first question focuses the potential reengineer on the need to define a vision and purpose for the organization, and it requires management to articulate and translate that vision into clear, achievable goals.

What Kind of Culture Do We Want?

The second question is about values, which translates into five essential work-related values: (1) to perform at the highest level of competency, (2) to take initiative and to risk, (3) to adapt to change, (4) to make decisions, and (5) to work as a team. There are also five essential human values: (1) to be open, (2) to trust and be trustworthy, (3) to respect others and oneself, (4) to accept responsibility, and (5) to be willing to judge and be judged, reward and be rewarded, based on performance.

In our view, the first two questions are really preparatory, prerequisites to reengineering, and at best guides to getting ready.

When the city of Indianapolis contemplated the reengineering of its workforce development programs in 1993, Mayor Goldsmith demanded that his key deputy on such matters, William B. Stephan, begin the project by developing measurable outcomes. Goldsmith and his team had come to appreciate the importance and difficulty of accessing comparable performance data in their efforts to contract out city services.

Values were an important consideration for Goldsmith and Stephan as they developed appropriate outcome measures. At the outset, they agreed that work was a fundamental value of the Indianapolis community. They therefore set a primary objective that every adult in the city had the right to expect an opportunity to engage in productive work, and at the same time the individual had the responsibility and obligation to take advantage of that work opportunity when it was provided. The central objective, then, of workforce development was simply to match people with jobs in Indianapolis and to stimulate the economy and train or retrain individuals to create jobs for those who could not find them.

The mayor and his staff agreed that a partnership among the three sectors—public, private, and nonprofit—was the best mechanism for creating a reengineered workforce development system emphasizing work instead of education and training. And they agreed that companies interested in providing workforce development services should compete among one another for that opportunity. Finally, the mayor decided that interested companies should be paid for performance only—that is, for their success in matching job seekers with available jobs.

With the mayor's support, Stephan embarked on what became a yearlong research and strategic planning process. CEOs from large and small companies, union leaders, representatives from the nonprofit sector, regional and state employment specialists, the religious community, local universities, and think tanks were all engaged. Stephan also drew on the information and experience provided by the mayor's privatization and competition advisory group known as SELTIC (Service, Efficiency and Lower Taxes for Indianapolis Committee). An outside consultant (Eimicke) was selected by the mayor and Stephan to provide objective analysis of the local situation and to add the experience of other, similarly situated localities to the decision-making process.

A report was completed and submitted to the mayor within six months. It recommended that the Private Industry Council's monopoly on workforce training and development programs in Indianapolis be replaced by a competitively bid, performance-based contract approach. The mayor and the Private Industry Council approved Stephan's plan, and an implementation committee of business leaders was established to make it happen. Six months later, the Private Industry Council was out of the training and placement business. A year later, Goodwill Industries outbid five other organizations (including a group of the former Private Industry Council employees and several national, for-profit placement firms) to operate the city's three one-stop employment centers.

Indianapolis has achieved substantial improvements in its workforce programs through reengineering, but it was reengineering that followed a rigorous effort at strategic planning, benchmarking, and outcomes identification. In the government's view, it did not make sense to totally redo the city's workforce development systems and processes before they first carefully considered what the existing processes were designed to achieve and what the desired outcomes for the future were.

How Does It Work?

The third question begins the actual reengineering process. The organization must begin by defining its objectives. Unlike followers of the management by objectives strategy, however, reengineers go beyond reasonable and realistic objectives and seek out radical, or at least very ambitious, targets.

The Minnesota Department of Revenue is responsible for administering the state's sales tax, an increasingly important source of revenue. By the early 1990s, the state's sales tax accounted for more than 25 percent of all state funds, totaling about $4 billion a year. Unfortunately, the state's sales tax computer system was more than twenty years old, and it was slow and increasingly vulnerable to inaccuracies. To justify the substantial cost of upgrading its computer system, the department decided to reengineer its sales tax collection processes. Among its most ambitious targets were making electronic filing an option for 90 percent of its customers, having accurate taxpayer registration and profiling within thirty days of customers' first reporting, and resolving all accounts receivable within ninety days. Full implementation was projected to yield the state in excess of $55 million in new revenues.

Reengineers measure performance in terms of "results for customers—their pleasure and/or pain" (National Academy of Public Administration, 1994, p. 122). The reengineered Minnesota sales tax collection process gave customers the new convenience of registering immediately at any department location, by telephone, or by fax. The information gathered was used to customize information packets to benefit the particular business involved and to notify its employees of appropriate training opportunities. Employees of the sales tax collection department are also empowered to make decisions to resolve tax issues and cases more quickly.

Reengineers must communicate the case for change—Why reengineer? How will success be measured? What steps will be taken? and How will those steps get us to the promised land? Communication was stressed throughout the Minnesota reengineering effort. Project managers kept the governor's office fully informed and up-to-date on the project's progress so that the governor's office could in turn make sure that the entire political network, the media, and the general public were kept in the loop. Internally, the department used Lotus Notes software to make sure that information was shared among the many teams working on the project.

With What Kind of People Do We Want to Work?

Unfortunately, advocates provide few suggestions for finding the right people or attracting them to one's reengineering project. Overall, reengineers focus on what do to but not on how to do it.

How to Do Reengineering

The first specific how-to guide appears in Michael Hammer and Steven Stanton's 1995 handbook on reengineering and encompasses six sequential steps:

1. *Mandate change.* Drive the process from the top down, with strong leadership, sustained commitment, and clear direction.

2. *Assemble the reengineering team.* To verify the importance of the project and assure optimal results, the organization's best and brightest must be assigned to the reengineering work. These talented individuals must be familiar with every aspect of the project to be reengineered.

3. *Understand the existing process and customer expectations.* You must know the process as it currently exists, in every detail; and you must identify the bottlenecks and obstacles and the unmet needs.

You must know from where you are jumping and you must have some idea of where you hope to land if a quantum leap forward is to be achieved.

4. *Invent the new process.* The new design must be developed in the context of uncertainty, experimentation, and pressure. The only certainty with which reengineering begins is that the current process is inadequate. Experimentation implies that new ways of working can be tested only on the ground, and that inevitably mistakes with real consequences will be made. Pressure comes from the reality that reengineering is often pursued to stave off imminent or looming demise. You must act first and then correct your mistakes as you go along. Benchmarking is appropriate here, as long as the new process builds in a quantum leap beyond the benchmark.

5. *Construct the new process.* A detailed operational plan must be developed that includes recruitment, training, and an information system.

6. *Sell the new process.* Just as with TQM, the new process behavior must rapidly become just "the way we do work around here." This includes overcoming the tremendous resistance to change and the comfort with the status quo that all organizations experience.

Although this approach is helpful, we do not believe it sufficiently differentiates reengineering from other innovation techniques, such as strategic planning and TQM, or that it provides sufficient guidance to the new reengineer. We suggest the following changes and additions to the six steps outlined by Hammer and Stanton:

1. Mandate change.
2. Hire a consultant.
3. Assemble the reengineering team.
4. Recognize, name, and understand the existing processes.
5. Ensure that all members know the processes and their importance.
6. Measure the processes.
7. Invent the new processes.

8. Construct the new processes.
9. Sell the new processes.
10. Strive for ongoing process improvement.

   1. *Mandate change.* This is carried on in the same manner as in Hammer and Stanton's step 1.
   2. *Hire a consultant.* Few reengineering efforts we know of have proceeded without consultant assistance. Because reengineering demands a radical break from the past, organizations usually need trained and committed outsiders to sustain their dedication to change. The significant role played by consultants is reinforced by estimates that in the mid-1990s, consultants accounted for about a third of the costs of reengineering.
   3. *Assemble the reengineering team.* Other than being moved one step further in the process, our only modification to Hammer's original direction is the addition of the reengineering consultant to the team.
   4. *Recognize, name, and understand the existing processes.* Identify and name all of the organization's key processes. For example, order fulfillment, product development, order acquisition, and other common work processes are present in most organizations. The typical organization has between five and fifteen key processes that must be identified, flowcharted, and named. This is no easy task, because processes cut across organizational lines and do not necessarily match up with existing functional units. To properly chart these processes, horizontal rather than top-down analysis is required.
   5. *Ensure that all members know the processes and their importance.* Everyone in the organization, from top to bottom, from head-quarters to the most far-flung outpost, must be aware of the organization's key processes. Employees are no longer workers completing isolated tasks. They are now performers, contributing their effort to the successful execution of an outcome-based process.
   6. *Measure the processes.* Management needs to know how well the organization's processes are performing, particularly if they are on the verge of reengineering those processes. Key measures should be based on what is important to the customer and should

generally be outcome-based. Other important measures relate to process cost, asset utilization, and efficiency assessments. Surely the organization wants to meet customer needs and desires, but if it can do so at a lower cost, so much the better. Measures chosen must also reflect the process as a whole and give everyone working on the process, as a team, a sense of how well they are performing.

7. *Invent the new processes.* This is carried on in the same manner as in Hammer and Stanton's step 4.

8. *Construct the new processes.* This is carried on in the same manner as in Hammer and Stanton's step 5.

9. *Sell the new processes.* This is carried on in the same manner as in Hammer and Stanton's step 6.

10. *Strive for ongoing process improvement.* Readers who are familiar with the original manifesto will find this direction quite surprising because reengineering was originally promoted as an antidote to the inherent weaknesses of incremental, continuous-improvement thinking. However, after nearly a decade of reengineering experience, observation, and analysis, Hammer (1996) concluded that "one shot improvements, even dramatic ones, are of little value" (p. 17). The heart of reengineering management is managing processes, assuring they are performing up to potential, looking for improvement opportunities and turning those opportunities into realities. Beyond reengineering is process-centered management, "a way of life" (p. 17).

What about making reengineering work in government—is it different? Yes, and based on our research on public organizations, in the United States and other countries, we find that the following four-step approach, developed by Russell Linden (1994) works best:

1. *Map the process as it currently exists.* This step typically begins with a flow chart of the current process. This "map" often makes it obvious that the organization does not take advantage of the current state-of-the-art information systems technology, and it identifies obvious bottlenecks and redundancies as well as efficient and effective processes. This step provides an essential baseline of time, cost, and quality, and a better understanding of how departments interact.

2. *Start at the end and work backward.* Begin this step by asking the end users or customers what they expect from the product or service to be delivered and then work backward to find the "leanest, most seamless process for providing that deliverable" (Linden, 1994, p. 142). Although this sounds like simple common sense, it is difficult to carry out in the real world of work. First, most organizational members see the work world only from the perspective of the role or task they play in it (such as, "Buddy, my job is to make sure you have the proper identification, not to help you make your flight!"). Also, customers do not always know exactly what they want. For example, people may know what they want their computers to do but they frequently do not know the command or the software that is both adequate and economical. And there may be a photographic or display application that they would love but they do not even know enough to ask about it. Effective definition of customer needs and desires takes close cooperation and trust between the user and the producer.

3. *Reach for the stars (but keep your feet on the ground)!* Perhaps the most quoted illustration of this step in the United States is former president John Kennedy's 1961 announcement of our collective goal of "putting a man on the moon and returning him safely to Earth, in this decade." Or the recruitment slogan of the U.S. Army: "Be all that you can be." The idea is to strive for a quantum leap in performance by getting everyone's attention, building enthusiasm and a can-do spirit, shattering constraining myths, and focusing on key customer-valued outcomes. Benchmarking against the best in the world or the best in your program area is essential to this exercise.

4. *Begin with a clean sheet.* This step begins with the simple directive to start over. A successful reengineering effort begins with a clean sheet and a clear plan. To be successful, the process to be reengineered must be driven by an outcomes-based strategy. That strategy could be as simple as "to become more customer-driven" or "to leverage our resources to help job seekers by partnering with community-based organizations." It makes little sense to improve the efficiency of a work process if an organization is not clear about what that process is designed to accomplish. The starting-over methodology of reengineering has deep roots in U.S. history and

culture. From our founding by immigrants to the western migration, the New Deal, the New Frontier, and recently, the Clinton-Gore program to reinvent or redesign government, Americans are frequently looking to do better by starting fresh. Starting over is our national myth and it enables us to overcome obstacles and constraints with breakthrough thinking and innovative change.

Each organization will find it useful to tailor its reengineering effort to its particular culture and circumstances. It may therefore be best to take the most appropriate components from the two models we suggest or from other models you have seen and liked. There is no one best way, but there may well be a better way for your organization. We like the models presented here because they are both simple and complete and have proven effective in the organizations we have observed.

Benefits of Reengineering

Hammer, Champy, Linden, and other reengineering advocates begin and often rest their case for reengineering on the brief affirmation, "It works!" Advocates have chronicled the reengineering miracles at Ford Motor Company, Hallmark, Taco Bell, Bell Atlantic, Wisconsin Electric, Cigna Health Care, Arizona Public Service, Hewlett-Packard, NutraSweet, Amoco, Liberty Mutual, DePaul and Brandeis Universities, ShowTime Networks, Aetna Life and Casualty, GTE, Nordstrom, and Home Depot.

Nor are the success stories limited to the private sector. Successful reengineering efforts all over the United States and even in the United Kingdom include Royal Mail service, the U.S. Social Security Administration; the Kansas Board of Education; several state government agencies in Arizona; the Army Corps of Engineers; NASA; the U.S. Department of Housing and Urban Development; the U.S. Internal Revenue Service; several agencies in Minnesota, Phoenix, and Arizona; Connecticut's Department of Labor; and the U.S. Department of Defense. The list of success stories is long and diverse, and spans nearly a decade.

But how exactly does reengineering improve the organization? What specifically can a manager expect to gain for the investment and risk? On the basis of their firsthand study of thirty-five public organizations, NAPA concluded that "the results are dramatic" (1994, p. ix). They listed substantial reductions in cycle time, lower production costs, greater productivity, and better quality products and services as typical reengineering outcomes.

In the private sector, proponents argue that reengineering is more than beneficial—it is essential for organizational survival in the new world of international competition and rapid innovation. It enables organizations to take risks, adapt, and change. It encourages and takes advantage of individual creativity.

Work and the way it is accomplished changes in a reengineered environment. The beneficial changes include the following:

1. There is a shift from functional organization to process teams.
2. Jobs change from simple tasks to multidimensional work.
3. People are empowered instead of controlled.
4. Performance evaluation and pay are based on results, not just on activity.

These changes are beneficial only to the extent that the organization produces desired outputs and outcomes—the quality of programs and services, customer satisfaction, efficiency, and improved morale. Proponents of reengineering argue that it will achieve all of the above and in quantum amounts above the preexisting baseline performance.

Costs of Reengineering

Reengineering is a high-cost, high-risk innovation strategy. Expensive outside consulting fees are only the beginning. Despite the success stories, many organizations achieve no improvement through reengineering and actually increase employee cynicism. Some reports estimate that between 50 and 70 percent of reengineering projects fail. The fear and subsequent dislocation caused by blank-sheet analysis often disrupts effective existing processes as well as those in need of and targeted for improvement. The entire organization's functioning may be impaired and slowed down during the reengineering project's life cycle.

While its advocates claim that reengineering is not downsizing, the elimination of many middle management jobs is a common by-product of the process. Those organizations that are interested only in downsizing frequently use a reengineering nameplate to add a scientific veneer to what are just layoffs. Reengineering and job loss are now so closely associated that many of an organization's best and most marketable people leave as soon as the word reengineering surfaces in the employee rumor mill.

Supporters also insist that reengineering is not reorganization. In practice, the costly and disruptive process of moving organizational boxes is common. We argue that for reengineering to be successful in the public sector, creation of an entirely new agency to house the redesigned process may be essential. Civil service, old-style public employee unions, and political forces within existing agencies can generally thwart major changes within an existing structure, particularly if headcount reductions and job reclassifications are involved.

Reengineering's laudable emphasis on holism and seamlessness can also be a limiting factor. Putting everything on the table can be daunting and can raise opposition from every corner of the agency and its concerned advocate community. Moreover, customers, competition, and technology are changing continuously as the reengineering revolution is implemented, which usually takes about a year. By the time the reengineering project is completed, changed circumstances or technology could dictate a second revolution. But can an organization function efficiently and retain its people in a constant state of reengineering?

Ideally, public sector reengineering would be accomplished through consensus and universal participation. But nonstop public and media pressure to reduce the cost and size of government just about guarantees that public sector reengineering will be primarily an exercise in downsizing. Radical redesign in the public sector is also constrained by partisan differences regarding government's mission, by short-term considerations driven by the next election, by legislative mandates, by policy differences between and among the three branches of government, by civil service restrictions, and by the opposition of some public employee unions. Nor are the resources always available in the public sector for hiring reengineering consultants and purchasing the equipment and information technology needed to implement some of the process change recommendations developed.

Many of the obstacles and constraints in regulation and law encountered in reengineering government exist for very good reasons—to protect the disadvantaged; to guard against waste, fraud, and abuse; to provide due process; or to prevent the tyranny of the majority. Advancing technology, changing social mores, and public education may mitigate the need for some government red tape over time, but public sector reengineers will usually have to be satisfied with less streamlining than is possible in the private sector.

Cynicism is an inevitable cost of reengineering, at least until it succeeds. Not only does the reengineering movement follow on the heels of two decades of successive silver-bullet management cure-alls—for example, Planning Programming Budgeting System, zero-based budgeting, management by objectives, Total Quality Management, and reinvention (Micklethwait and Wooldridge, 1996), to name just a few—but reengineering very frequently is launched in the face of an organizational crisis that will cost many current members their jobs. In the private sector this usually leads to turnover and a major blow to corporate spirit.

In the public sector, many middle managers and even higher-ups, protected by civil service or powerful friends, will wait out or even secretly sabotage the reengineering effort. Most government agency heads move up or out in the time it takes to mount and implement a reengineering project. That is why we believe that for reengineering to be successful in the public sector, the creation of a new organizational unit or even an entirely new agency may be required.

Reengineering has attracted a great deal of media attention and many true believers, and has helped organizations from all three sectors survive and prosper. At the same time, as even its strongest advocates repeat again and again, reengineering is not easy, cheap, or quick, and comes with no guarantee of success. We are convinced that reengineering is not most effective as a stand-alone innovation strategy. The most successful reengineering projects are preceded by an effective strategic planning exercise, guided by a formal benchmarking effort, implemented by workers organized into teams, accomplished at least in part through privatization (outsourcing parts of the process that suppliers or customers can do better or more cheaply), and kept on the cutting edge through continuous improvement (TQM). In other words, reengineering is an even bigger undertaking for an organization than it appears to be on the surface, and it will not be easily or quickly carried out.

Reengineers are probably best advised not to go too far in their efforts to disassociate themselves from downsizing. Our review indicates that a reduction in the number of jobs, particularly at the middle management level, is almost always a by-product of a reengineering exercise. The typical organization of the twenty-first century will have only one-third the managers of the late-twentieth-century model. The responsibilities of those to-be-downsized managers are taken over by already-present knowledge workers, utilizing the ever-improving tools of information technology.

This rather large, across-the-board reduction in the management ranks is necessary and unavoidable because these managers neither make decisions nor lead. Their function has been to relay information, and they are therefore easily replaced by knowledge workers using information technology to provide the information directly to top managers who make key decisions. We believe, therefore, that effective reengineering requires the mastery and marriage of the innovation strategies described in this book and that it is inexorably tied to a reduction in the number of managers. A more positive observation is that it will probably also result in better, more empowered workers who can increase their pay, power, and prestige by advancing "in place." In that sense, many organizations may become more like sports and entertainment organizations in which talented workers often make much more than their bosses, have more marketable skills, and are encouraged to get better at what they do best, rather than seek rewards through climbing the organizational hierarchy.

Is reengineering, then, any more than intelligent downsizing and hierarchy flattening? We think so. Reengineering incorporates a new way of thinking about management innovation and change—it encourages thinking big, creativity, breakthrough methodology, and quantum leaps. In our view, successful reengineering requires the support of other innovative strategies to maximize its benefits, and a commitment to continuous improvement to sustain its gains. Used appropriately, with the necessary investment of time, equipment, technology, and patience, reengineering has produced major gains and sustained those improvements over long periods.

Chapter Four

| Total Quality Management

Total Quality Management (TQM) is a fundamental approach to how work gets done within an organization. As a management approach, TQM can be reduced to three central elements (Cohen and Brand, 1993).

1. *Collaboration with suppliers to ensure that the supplies utilized in work processes are well designed and fit for use* is essential to the quality process primarily because it can prevent problems from occurring. If issues are addressed in the "upstream" stages of the production process, then inspections, reworkings, and responding to customer complaints "downstream" becomes unnecessary (Swiss, 1992, p. 357).

2. *Continuous employee analysis of work processes to improve their functioning and reduce process variation* ensures that those with the most intimate knowledge of how an organization's work gets done are contributing to the organization's quest for high-quality outputs.

3. *Close communication with customers to identify and understand what they want and how they define quality* is important to the quality organization because for any organization customer satisfaction is the ultimate determinant of success. To be successful, organizations must meet and exceed the expectations of their customers; that is why continual communication with customers aimed at discerning their definition of quality is crucial to the TQM process.

Exhibit 4.1 presents an operational definition of TQM by detailing the steps involved in any TQM process.

**Exhibit 4.1. The Operational Steps in
Total Quality Management.**

Step 1   Have the workers describe and measure their work and identify the work processes that should be improved.

Step 2   Describe the steps involved in performing the work. (Who does what? When?)

Step 3   Identify the places in the process that most frequently create defects, delays, and rework.

Step 4   Identify the causes of defects, delays, and rework. These can include poor equipment, inappropriate or unclear instructions, inadequate standard operating procedures, poor direction and communication, or inadequately trained workers and managers.

Step 5   Experiment with small-scale pilot projects designed to improve the process.

Step 6   If the pilot tests work, institute the changed procedure throughout the organization.

Step 7   Monitor the new process to be sure that it helps improve performance over time.

Step 8   Repeat steps 1 through 7 and continuously improve performance.

How TQM Works

On the basis of our years of experience with and research on public sector management techniques, we have identified two general versions of TQM. One approach that we have developed and implemented successfully in public and nonprofit organizations is what we call *project-oriented TQM*. The other approach is the traditional and probably more common TQM approach, which we have taken to calling *consultant-driven TQM*.

Traditional (Consultant-Driven) TQM

This is the formal brand of TQM that is based on taking W. Edwards Deming's prescriptions verbatim and then attempting to bring them into a traditional organization. We call this consultant-driven TQM because as near as we can see the consultants hired to implement TQM according to the traditional approach appear to be the primary beneficiaries of this process.

The traditional model follows Deming's edict to obtain commitment from the "top" of the organization. It involves massive and rapid training of the entire organization in TQM tools and group process skills. It requires the establishment of a quality council, quality coordinators, quality work plans, and quality souvenir merchandise.

According to our experience in the field, consultant-driven TQM usually results in a quality shadow organization that approves improvement projects, supervises quality teams, and is coordinated by a team of TQM managers. This quality organization exists separately from the traditional organizational structure and chain of command. In organizational terms, this can have one of three results: (1) eventually the traditional structure reasserts itself and eliminates the quality organization, (2) the quality organization takes over, or (3) everyone gets confused and productivity declines as the two separate structures compete for resources, loyalty, and important assignments.

Clearly we believe that this traditional model for implementing TQM is problematic in general and particularly so in the public and nonprofit sectors. In government, accountability is critical and a single chain of command is essential. In both government and the nonprofit sector the absence of a bottom line makes it difficult to stay focused. The emergence of the separate, quality-specific organizational structure often engendered by traditionally implemented TQM only makes matters worse.

Moreover, we have observed that in government the traditional hierarchy always dominates the quality organization set up by consultants and human resource shops; this means that ultimately the traditional TQM initiative fails to integrate itself into the operations of the traditional organizational structure. Proof of this finding is illustrated in what we call the Mayor's Fire Drill. The Mayor's Fire Drill is a good litmus test for assessing to what extent the quality organization has integrated itself into the traditional structure and chain of command of the organization. The test goes like this: When the mayor calls the commissioner and says, "We have an emergency on our hands," who does the commissioner call? The first deputy for operations, or the head of the quality council? As we're sure you have guessed, the commissioner usually contacts the operations chief. Moreover, if the work involved in the emergency conflicts with a meeting of the quality council or a quality team, quality is always tossed out the window.

Unless TQM is quickly seen as "the normal way we work around here," it becomes irrelevant and trivialized. The best way to ensure that TQM succeeds is to integrate it into the normal operations and routines of the organization. This means that TQM must be adapted to the culture of the organization rather than adapting the culture to TQM. Colin Morgan and Stephen Murgatroyd (1994, p. 6) agree: "TQM is user-driven, it cannot be imposed from outside the organization. . . . TQM is concerned chiefly with changing attitudes and skills so that the culture of the organization becomes one of preventing failure—doing things right, right first time, every time." Consultant-driven TQM fails to integrate TQM into the organization's culture. For TQM to be truly integrated, the organization must do its own customer, supplier, and work process analysis. Consultants are a crutch that the organization must discard before TQM becomes the manner in which it approaches its work.

In addition to these significant disadvantages, implementing TQM according to the traditional or consultant-driven model is very costly. The support costs of a traditional TQM effort are enormous and require many hours of high-priced talent with skills in statistical process control and group dynamics.

Outside consultants have an important but very limited role to play in bringing about organizational change. They can present new ideas and give organizations ideas based on the experiences of other organizations. They can provide staff support for innovation initiatives. However, the goal of any innovation consultant must be to quickly train internal leaders or change agents to adapt and carry the message further within the organization. If consultants do not help organizations to develop this self-sufficiency, the change process will tend to be superficial and short-lived. Change-oriented consultants must leave the organization relatively quickly in order for change to take root.

Ultimately, many high-priced billable hours are used in consultant-driven TQM processes to force-feed TQM practices that an organization will never accept. The lesson is that organizations are far too complicated to accept verbatim any consultant's or TQM guru's formula for success. To genuinely change the organization's approach to work and eventually ensure ever-higher quality levels in organizational outputs, the quality process must be carefully crafted and implemented according to the unique needs of the organization. Consultant-driven TQM fails to take this necessity into account.

Project-Oriented TQM

In response to the shortcomings of TQM as traditionally implemented, we have developed a government-oriented adaptation that we call project-oriented TQM. It includes the following elements:

1. *A focus on production in the field.* Management and workers should focus their attention on the process of producing goods and services. Understanding exactly what happens when work is performed is an essential element of TQM. As noted by James Bowman (1994, p. 129), "According to TQM, problems do not originate with employees, but from a lack of understanding of the work processes. The TQM objective is to analyze processes to identify barriers to quality, satisfy internal and external beneficiaries of the work performed ('customers'), and create an atmosphere of continuous improvement." From this point of view, quality can be improved only after management and workers have completed a step-by-step description and analysis of the work process.

2. *Worker participation.* To increase the level of attention paid to production, management must depend on workers to analyze and suggest improvements to work processes. Because workers perform these tasks, only they have access to all the information about how work gets done. If management does not obtain this information, it is very difficult to improve quality.

3. *Communication with customers and suppliers.* Morgan and Murgatroyd (1994, p. 7) explain that "the TQM perspective considers that all people working within the organization—whether manufacturing, commercial service, or public sector provision—are linked in a network or *chain of customer-supplier relationships*. Hence, the intent of TQM is that all internal customers are to be equally well satisfied with the service or product they are supplied with as

are the external or end-user customers to be." This observation illustrates the importance of continual communication with suppliers as well as with customers.

To improve quality, a worker must have supplies that are well designed and fit for use, and suppliers must learn to tailor their supplies to the needs of particular production processes. Supplies can include computer equipment, forms, or directions from a supervisor. Similarly, to determine what customers want and how customers define quality, an organization must constantly be learning their customers' preferences. As noted earlier, the customer is the ultimate determiner of an organization's success in providing quality outputs.

4. *Rapid changes in standard operating procedures and constant training.* TQM requires that organizations constantly analyze and change work processes. Continuous improvement requires continuous modification of standard operating procedures and the communication of those new processes throughout the organization. For an organization to be flexible and adaptable, it is important for managers and workers to analyze work processes and collaborate without fear, and without worrying whether mistakes discovered in the analysis process will be punished (Swiss, 1992).

5. *Small-scale projects.* To teach workers how to communicate with suppliers and customers and analyze their own work processes, it is best to start with small, easy-to-understand aspects of the organization's daily work. This process quickly builds a record of visible accomplishments and avoids misinterpreting boundary disputes as TQM failures. One of the best ways to learn is by doing, and the best way to learn by doing is to start with something manageable that has a high probability of success.

6. *Eventual invisibility.* Eventually, TQM becomes simply "the way we work around here." In our experience, this typically takes a few years, and the time frame varies according to the size and type of organization. We agree with Daniel Hunt (1993, p. 3), who writes that "quality management is not so much a specific set of activities as it is a management approach"—that is, a way of doing work. It is necessary for TQM to become the organization's way of operating because quality requires continuous improvement and because "quality is not a static attribute" (Swiss, 1992, p. 357)—that is, the definition of quality itself will change over time. The goal is

for everyone in the organization to view communication with customers and suppliers and analysis of work processes as the normal way of approaching any task.

7. *Use of existing departmental procedures and structures as a foundation.* With any organizational change, it makes sense to build on what already is working well. Therefore, when an organization undertakes TQM it should reinforce the importance of TQM through routine management processes. Managers should ask, What do the customers think? How is this job done now? and so on. This will help the organization to avoid establishing a shadow quality organization that exists solely to implement quality improvement projects and that does not integrate itself into the existing organizational structure and operation.

In addition to these recommendations, we have developed a checklist (Exhibit 4.2) that details the steps involved in implementing project-oriented TQM. The checklist is drawn from our earlier work in TQM (Cohen and Brand, 1993; Cohen and Eimicke, 1995). It has been field-tested in more than a dozen public, nonprofit, and private organizations. One way to go through the checklist is to try to project how you would answer each of the checklist questions for a sample project.

1. *What activity is the project seeking to improve?* This is the substantive area you are working on. An example of a general work activity you may seek to improve is decreasing the number of errors on biweekly paychecks. Within this general activity, many specific, component tasks occur, which are identified by checklist item 3.

2. *Who is the project's team leader and who are the team's members?* Ideally, management should consult with the team leader when forming the team. In some cases, it is necessary for management simply to designate a team leader and to tell that leader who will be on the team. If the unit head and the team leader are involved in selecting the team (typically a good idea) then a number of issues should be discussed.

• Who undertakes the work you are seeking to improve? Make sure that someone involved in all crucial elements of the work is on the team.

Exhibit 4.2. Quality Improvement Project Checklist.

1. What activity is the project seeking to improve?
2. Who is the project's team leader and who are the team's members?
3. What specific work process are you trying to improve?
4. How is this work process now performed?
5. What is the current level of performance of this work process?
6. How have you measured the level of performance?
7. What additional information or data do you need to measure the current level of performance more precisely?
8. How do you plan to collect or obtain this information?
9. What will you do with this information once you have collected it?
10. What are the most significant obstacles to improving this work process?
11. Identify one (or possibly two) of these significant obstacles and develop a method for overcoming it.
12. Develop a pilot project to try out the work process improvement.

    • What changes in procedure are you planning to institute? How is the activity now done? How will it change?
    • Who will manage and staff the pilot project?
    • How long will the project last?
    • What is the definition of success?
    • Who will decide whether to institute the change throughout the organization?

13. To what degree has the pilot project improved the level of performance?

    • How are you measuring improvement?
    • How will you translate the improvement into an estimate of dollar or other savings?
    • What are the annual savings resulting from this project?

• Who are the suppliers and customers for the work (internal and external)? Is it possible to include these customers or suppliers on the team? If not, they should be consulted as part of the team's work.
• Is there a good mix of skills and levels of seniority on the team?

3. *What specific work process are you trying to improve?* When first undertaking TQM, people frequently confuse the general activity they are seeking to improve (checklist item 1) with the specific work process they are trying to improve. This item is included in the checklist to focus the team on actual work processes.

To improve work, project teams must know what specific work process, or tasks, they are trying to improve. Let's say that to improve the accuracy of paychecks, you decided to focus on reducing the frequency of errors made in time card submission. In this case, filling out, transmitting, and receiving the time card are three specific work processes you seek to improve. These processes in turn affect the accuracy of time cards, which subsequently affects the accuracy of paychecks, which are disbursed on the basis of information contained on the time cards.

4. *How is this work process now performed?* Once you know what you are trying to improve, you must begin to describe how it is performed. This description is best thought of as a series of discrete steps. In general, the best method for describing work is to construct a flowchart of all the steps involved in doing a job. Answer the questions, Who does what? and When? Describe what *actually* happens, not what *should* happen. One purpose of the flowchart is to identify the different ways that people do the same job. Some fairly easy improvements can be found by learning what others do. The purpose of the flowchart is not to discover the right way and the wrong way to do a job, but simply to describe the various ways that a single job is accomplished.

5. *What is the current level of performance of this work process?* Once you know how a job is done, the next question to address is how to measure the performance of the job. How often is this process done? What are the results of this job? How much is produced through this process? How often is rework required? How high is the quality of the output of this process? It is difficult to improve something if you do not have a baseline measure of current performance. Without the baseline measurement, you have no way of knowing whether you are improving or not. If no baseline data exist, the first step is to take time out to gather the data.

6. *How have you measured the level of performance?* This question directs you to ask the team to search for currently collected data

that can shed insight on the current level of performance. Is there regular reporting on standard forms? Is this information collected and totaled in a report? Has anyone conducted a short-term study of this activity? Do managers or workers have guesstimates on the current level of performance?

7. *What additional information or data do you need to more precisely measure the current level of performance?* In many cases, you will find that the activity the team is trying to improve is not being measured and that some form of additional information is needed. This question directs you to think about the type of information you need to determine your current level of performance. If you were trying to improve the maintenance of vehicles, you might want to measure (1) the number of times per year the vehicle is inspected, (2) the condition and age of the vehicle, (3) the number of repairs and parts replaced in a given period, and (4) the amount of time it takes to process a request for a repair or replacement. The team might also identify other factors involving vehicle maintenance as important. This is the point in the quality improvement process at which to identify information needed to get to the probable cause of the problem you are examining.

8. *How do you plan to collect or obtain this information?* Once the team has decided on the type of information it needs, it must then develop a method for collecting the information. One typical method is to develop a reporting form to be filled out by workers involved in doing the work. If this is done, it is important that people be trained to fill out the form, and that the team develop a regular method of collecting completed forms. It is critical that the information collected be necessary, and that data collection be as simple and painless as possible. It is important that the people who fill out the form understand why they are filling it out. Before people are asked to fill out a form they should be asked to comment on it and improve it if possible.

9. *What will you do with this information once you have collected it?* Do not collect any information that you do not absolutely need to measure and improve performance. Before you collect the information, make sure that your team is completely clear about how they will use the information and about what they are hoping to learn. We suggest that when new information is being collected you

collect it for a week as a pilot experiment and then create a sample report describing the current level of performance. If the information is useful, continue to collect it; if it is not, stop collecting it and try something else.

It is important to make the collected data available to those who can use it to improve work processes. In her case study of implementing TQM in the Internal Revenue Service, Bonnie Mani (1995) explains that data was collected, summarized, and distributed to those who could use it. Some data were made part of a display containing charts and illustrations. The means for distributing work process data will vary from organization to organization; the important thing is that the information be readily available and easy to use.

10. *What are the most significant obstacles to improving this work process?* Once you have described how the work gets done and have measured the current work process and what it produces, you are ready to identify where the problems are. This involves analyzing the information on hand, brainstorming with the team, and thinking about where inefficient or illogical work steps might be. Often it is useful to look at the amount of time particular steps take and see whether it might be improved.

You should use the flowchart of the work activity as a starting point for this analysis. Look at each step in the work and help the team to rank order which of these steps seems to have the most problems. Once you have performed this ranking, you are ready for the next stage of the quality improvement project.

11. *Identify one (or possibly two) of these significant obstacles and develop a method for overcoming it.* At this point you are ready to focus your project on one aspect of the work you wish to improve. Perhaps some step or steps in the process can be eliminated. Perhaps you have learned a way that the work is done differently in another organization. It may be that the team has thought of a new way the work could be done. At this stage in the improvement project you want to identify a method for overcoming the obstacle on which the team is focusing. You need to work with your group to come up with at least one method for overcoming the obstacle they ranked as most significant, or for overcoming the second most significant obstacle, if the top obstacle seems too tough to take on.

12. *Develop a pilot project to try out the work process improvement.* Now the team is ready to propose to management a pilot quality project. The team should create a brief (one- or two-page) project proposal that identifies the following:

- The changes in work procedures that are planned
- How the work is now done and how it will change
- The manager of the pilot project
- The project's schedule, start date, and end date
- How the project's success or failure will be measured, including the data to be collected and the definition of success

If your supervisor approves, the pilot project should begin. It should be of limited duration, with a clear end point at which to analyze its success.

13. *To what degree has the pilot project improved the level of performance?* To answer this question, the team must assess how the project has changed the way the work is done and what impact the project has had on specific performance measures. When the pilot project is over, the team should develop a brief report of the project's costs and benefits. On the basis of that report, management should decide whether to continue the new work process and perhaps expand it to other locations, or to terminate the new process.

Remember that not all pilot projects succeed. It is OK if the project does not work, but it is not OK if results are distorted because you are afraid to fail. Sometimes you try something and it fails. The best thing to do in that case is to end the pilot project and try another. When a project works, the team should not automatically disband; additional improvements should be suggested and the team should either continue or be reconstituted to work on the next improvement. Quality improvement should be continuous and never-ending.

We have now introduced you to our approach to TQM: project-oriented TQM. In our minds and supported by our experiences in the field, this approach to TQM has a higher probability of success than traditionally oriented TQM, and it is more apt to allow for the genuine integration of the TQM approach into the organization's daily operations. Project-oriented TQM allows an organization to learn TQM by doing; it also creates an environment ripe for a quick TQM success and lays the foundation of skills and processes to expand that success to other projects across the organization.

Benefits of TQM

TQM enables an organization to tap into knowledge about work processes possessed only by workers. It empowers staff to think and it can enhance morale. Mani (1995, drawing on the work of Gibbons, 1993) considers TQM's morale-enhancing effect in terms of internal customers: "Internal customers are beneficiaries when the stress of poor work relationships is reduced, communications are improved, and employees are empowered to make decisions. The organization subsequently benefits with improved productivity" (p. 157). TQM can result in higher quality and lower cost production as work steps are rationalized and supplies are improved (Hiam, 1993). It provides a means for bringing customer preferences into an organization, for increasing the organization's ability to deliver what its customers want.

TQM is perhaps particularly timely for the public sector. Hunt (1993, p. 45), for example, believes that TQM responds to a "crisis of survival" that is now confronting the public sector: "In light of severe budget cutbacks, government managers are pressed to carry out their current missions more effectively. But if anything, the demand for quality government service is increasing."

We believe that in addition to these advantages one of TQM's main benefits is that it provides a vehicle for utilizing the brain power of everyone in the organization. Bowman (1994) points out that the only sustainable advantage an organization has is its people. Though "planning, organizing, staffing, and directing take place by promoting teamwork, coaching, listening, and leading," TQM ensures that an organization leverages its "only sustainable advantage" strategically and in order to improve organizational outputs (p. 137). As production becomes more information based and flexible and less mechanical, organizations need to become more agile and thoughtful.

We also believe that people increasingly expect to participate in decisions in the workplace. They are less willing simply to accept top-down decisions; instead, they must be convinced of the logic of these decisions. TQM provides a structured means of eliciting the expertise, knowledge, and views of workers in the workplace, without the complications of true workplace democracy.

Costs of TQM

Perhaps the most difficult challenge to overcome in the implementation of TQM is the resistance to change that tends to be a part of human nature. According to Mani's (1995) research, "Resistance to change is a common problem in organizations that adopt the total quality management philosophy" (p. 148). What is more, both Mani and Morgan and Murgatroyd (1994) find that the resistance to change may be even greater in public organizations whose operations are constrained by a myriad of rules, regulations, and standard operating procedures. We believe that this resistance to change can be overcome if the TQM initiative involves changes that lessen operational challenges and improve organizational functioning and performance.

Once human nature is overcome, a number of obstacles to the successful implementation of TQM remain. First and foremost, if the organization's overall strategy is faulty, TQM will have the effect of improving production of the wrong thing. Furthermore, if standard private sector TQM is applied unmodified in government, too much will be tried too soon and the effort will probably fail. In our view, project-oriented TQM is a more appropriate solution for the public sector because it recognizes the fact that government organizations are characterized by independent power bases. The leaders of these powerful independent units must be recruited to TQM; they cannot be forced to comply, as they are with traditionally implemented TQM.

It is difficult to fire these managers; they cannot be swept aside by the top-level leadership, as called for by Deming in his version of TQM. Although "demonstrated commitment of top-level management is critical to the successful implementation of TQM," if *middle managers* do not support TQM, they will simply wait out the transitory elected and appointed officials championing the initiative and kill it at the first opportunity (Mani, 1995, p. 148). Jonathan Walters (1994b) agrees that a significant challenge to implementing TQM in the public sector is the transitory nature and short time horizon of elective politics.

Another cost of TQM in the public sector has to do with the difficulty of reconciling the claims of competing or contradictory customer demands. Unlike the private sector, the government cannot simply decide that it intends to serve only a market niche. Sometimes the people who supply the resources for a service are not the direct users of the service. This means you will have one set of customers paying for and another set of customers receiving a particular service. For example, taxpayers pay for welfare programs, but welfare recipients (who may or may not be taxpayers) actually use welfare services.

The members of this heterogeneous customer base may define quality service differently (Morgan and Murgatroyd, 1994). As Swiss (1992) points out, this differing definition of quality could relate, for example, to the level of resources that different people feel should be devoted to the provision of a given service: "The buying customers (general taxpayers) will often prefer to minimize costs. At the same time, the direct customers (recipients) of such programs may expect a level of quality that is found only at a very high price" (p. 359).

Another significant challenge for public managers attempting to implement TQM is that it fundamentally changes their role. Morgan and Murgatroyd (1994, p. 177) find that "as empowerment and self-management grows within the organization, managers need to accept significant role changes and a higher degree of risk." Managers become facilitators instead of field generals—supervising the independent efforts of empowered individuals.

Finally, any organization undertaking to make TQM "the way we work around here" must accept that genuine cultural change will not happen overnight. "Unlike mechanical fixes, cultural change takes time and is hard work. . . . Experience shows that it takes years to create a new environment, or culture, that places a premium on excellence; to build structures that will sustain and manage change; and to build an education system to support the expanded role for workers" (Hunt, 1993, p. 32). In our experience, it takes approximately five to ten years for TQM to take root fully in an organization.

Despite these challenges, we believe that TQM is, quite simply, the best way to work. Ensuring that supplies are fit for use improves the production process and eliminates problems before they occur. Consulting with workers, who understand work processes intimately, makes managers privy to important information that can improve operations and the quality of outputs. Continuous communication with customers ensures that the organization is producing what its customers desire; pleasing customers is the only way to achieve true success. Given these results, we find it difficult to imagine why anyone would argue against implementing TQM in the public sector.

Chapter Five

Benchmarking and Performance Management

The term *benchmarking* comes from the land surveyor's practice of making a mark on a rock or structure to serve as a common reference point, or benchmark, from which other measurements can be made. When benchmarking was first introduced as a management innovation strategy in the late 1970s, practitioners and academics were generally unimpressed. Common responses included, "I knew that!" "We do that all the time!" or "Why, that's just common sense."

In many respects, we agree—benchmarking is basically applied common sense. Many successful people and organizations do it intuitively. Good teachers, trainers, and mentors have preached its virtues for generations, while not calling it by the same name. However, while benchmarking may be common sense, it is not uniformly applied in large organizations.

To us, benchmarking is best defined as "simply the systematic process of searching for best practices, innovative ideas and highly effective operating procedures that lead to superior performance" (Bogan and English, 1994, p. 11). Not only does each person's creativity have limits, but the realities of our global village and new forms of communication (such as the Internet and World Wide Web) document daily that there is an almost limitless supply of new, good ideas out there. And as one person publicizes his or her good idea, hundreds of others are quickly at work adapting it to their needs and environment and making the technique even more effective.

Some have said that the first benchmarker was the second person to light a fire. In more recent times we could look at Henry Ford's adaptation of the Chicago slaughterhouse meat processing system to the fledgling automobile industry, or at Remington Rifle Company's study of Maybelline's lipstick case production to find a way to meet its customers' demand for shinier bullets.

Industry was using benchmarking techniques for decades before it became a self-conscious practice. It was done in practice long before it was named and taught consciously. It was either known as *copying* or, in its worst form, *industrial espionage*. Only recently have management experts begun to codify the technique and apply it systematically. It is rather surprising that benchmarking took so long to catch on as a management innovation strategy. Only in the 1970s did benchmarking begin to show up in normal business practice as a performance enhancement technique. At that time, it consisted of simply comparing one's business performance with that of one's direct competitors.

In the early 1980s, the Xerox Corporation, under the leadership of CEO David Kearns, became the most visible and influential proponent of benchmarking as a path to performance improvement. The Xerox approach involved comparing their products, services, and practices with those of their toughest competitors. This approach, which was the model for benchmarking in the 1980s, appears rather narrow from today's perspective because it is focused only on the end results of direct competitors.

Today, successful benchmarkers recognize that change is ever more rapid; that customers are more sophisticated, worldly, and demanding; and that good ideas can be found and adapted from almost anywhere. Benchmarkers can also alert the organization to fundamental changes in its industry, the environment, or the global landscape that are likely to affect the organization's business. Change is difficult for any organization, and there is frequently a tendency to focus inward to avoid seeing innovations that will force fundamental change in the way the organization functions. Benchmarking helps to guard against this avoidance reflex.

Benchmarking did not enter the government management innovation dialogue until the 1990s, but it became very popular very quickly. By 1994, *Governing* magazine was writing about the "benchmarking craze" (Walters, 1994a). That benchmarking was so rapidly and widely embraced by public managers should not come as a surprise. The pressure to do more with less—sparked by the local tax cuts mandated in the 1970s Proposition 13 in California, the Thatcher-Reagan antigovernment movement of the 1980s, and the deficit reduction and global competition spirit of the 1990s—continues to escalate.

We think that public managers embrace benchmarking more readily than they embrace other management innovation techniques developed in the private sector because they see it as a process of peer comparison. They can look to other governments rather than to the private sector to evaluate themselves and learn new methods. We think that this sector-limited benchmarking is too narrow, but it has at least encouraged many public managers to look beyond their own government to measure success and find better ways of working.

Searching for best practices is common to most definitions of benchmarking, whether public or private sector oriented. The definitions vary significantly in terms of the suggested comparison group, ranging from direct competitors to the best in the industry, the best in the region, the best in the nation, the best in the world, or even just the best in your own organization. While benchmarking sounds simple and is spreading rapidly, this is no guarantee that it will work for your organization (Biesada, 1991).

Measuring the performance of government agencies to improve their efficiency has a long history, although it has not always been known as benchmarking. In the 1970s, the International City and County Managers Association issued a 1974 report, *Measuring the Effectiveness of Basic Municipal Services*, which presented a series of measures that local governments might use to monitor their own performance and evaluate how well they were doing.

Although W. Edwards Deming's writings went largely unnoticed in his U.S. homeland until the mid-1980s, the use of statistical performance measurement and control chart benchmarking" that he advocated has been broadly applied in the public and private sectors in Japan and elsewhere since the late 1940s. The Japanese practice of finding and adapting the best of the best *(dantotsu)* is benchmarking, pure and simple.

The work of the Hoover Commissions in the 1950s to improve the economy and efficiency of federal agencies of the U.S. government derived many of its improvement recommendations by looking at best practices in the leading public and private organizations of the day. In the 1990s, the work of the National Performance Review (NPR) directed by Vice President Al Gore was primarily a reinvention exercise. Yet a rereading of David Osborne and Ted Gaebler's *Reinventing Government* (1992) and of the original NPR report (Gore, 1993) reveals a common use of best-practice modeling as the path to performance improvement. That is, there is a great deal of overlap between benchmarking and reinvention. Osborne and Peter Plastrik define *reinvention* as "the fundamental transformation of public systems and organizations to create dramatic increases in their effectiveness, efficiency, adaptability and capacity to innovate" (1997, pp. 13–14). Reinvention calls for flatter organizational hierarchies with fewer levels of decision making and greater empowerment and discretion for employees. Organizations seeking a "fundamental transformation" frequently use benchmarking.

Performance measurement as a means of assessing relative effectiveness, spurring improvements, and making resource allocation decisions has also been part of the public budgeting practice and literature since at least the 1960s. Former U.S. Secretary of Defense Robert McNamara brought the performance-based budgeting system from the private sector to the Kennedy administration. President Carter's zero-based budgeting was also rooted in performance measurement and benchmarking government agencies against one another. And the 1993 Government Results and Performance Act requires federal agencies to establish explicit strategic plans and performance goals and to report to Congress on their success in meeting the benchmarks they set for themselves before new appropriations are made. Developing numerical answers to the question, How well are we doing? in terms of economy and efficiency is the essence of "budget benchmarking" (Grifel, 1993).

To succeed, a benchmarking program must be founded on organizational consensus around several key components:

1. The best measurable indicators of the organizations' most important products, services, and processes
2. A widely accepted measure or yardstick through which the organization's performance can be compared with the performance of other organizations that are doing the same thing

3. Consensus around the desired benchmark standard—"best in our field," "best in the region," "best in the country," or "best in the world"
4. Agreement on the criteria and procedure through which the best will be identified and compared

Systematic benchmarking and performance measurement are necessarily intertwined but are not different names for the same procedure (although they are often incorrectly used interchangeably). Performance measurement is the process by which key measurable surrogates for the organization's most important processes, outputs, and outcomes are agreed upon and measured. These measures then serve as the basis or baseline on which internal and external comparisons can be made.

Once a baseline is established, benchmarking can begin. Benchmarking involves the identification of those organizations whose performance you hope to match and ultimately surpass. Next, you must seek to understand why the other organization's performance exceeds that of your organization, and how you might import their superior methods and processes to your organization. Frequently, improvement of a series of indicators will be required to achieve the desired higher level of performance.

Measurement is essential to successful benchmarking, but the quantitative aspects of the technique should be used with the cautions that no data are perfect, few comparisons are exactly on target, and too much meaning is often given to relatively insignificant statistical variation. "Done incorrectly, benchmarking produces reams of data and little else" (Bruder and Gray, 1994, p. 9). Analysts often fall back on measures that are easy to define and collect.

Benchmarking can produce dramatic improvements relatively quickly and inexpensively. It can also be easy to understand and apply. But benchmarking must be conducted in a careful and systematic fashion if it is to be effective.

How Benchmarking Works

Similar to reengineering, benchmarking has proven more difficult to apply than it is to describe. As with reengineering and TQM, line managers often undertake a benchmarking project by concentrating on a specific benchmark or metric that compares their current level of performance (or achievement) with that of their chief competitor.

The benchmarking objective can also be too broad or general—such as, let's become the best in the business. Are we dedicated to feeding the hungry and housing the homeless or are we in the job placement business? And how do we measure success? Is our organization about making home appliances or are we a computer maker or do we manage telecommunications? Is our objective immediate profit or long-term market share? Is it numbers of people sheltered and fed for the night or is it numbers of apartments built to rent at affordable rates?

Too many indicators are frequently identified, confusing the team and making the task overly time-consuming and complex. Choosing too many indicators is usually the result of concentrating on too many operations or organizational processes simultaneously. Finally, best-in-class organizations are often chosen on the basis of their reputation or advertising instead of their documented best practices. Such mistakes are common in initial benchmarking efforts but are easily correctable, and there are several excellent benchmarking process models to assist an organization in getting on the right track.

In our view, there is no one best model of benchmarking processes. You should choose the model that makes most sense to you and seems to fit your particular circumstances best. We will suggest several models for consideration that have worked well for others in both the public and private sectors.

The following very popular, simple, and easy-to-apply five-step approach is used by many companies, including the Baldrige Award-winning Motorola Company:

1. Decide what to benchmark.
2. Identify appropriate organizations to benchmark against.
3. Gather data.
4. Analyze the data and integrate them into an action plan.
5. Recalibrate and recycle the process.

More complicated but equally popular is the nine-step approach used by, among others, two-time Baldrige winner AT&T:

1. Identify what to benchmark.
2. Develop a benchmarking plan.
3. Choose a data collection method.
4. Collect data.
5. Choose best-in-class companies.
6. Collect data on site visits to the best-in-class.
7. Compare processes, identify gaps, and develop recommendations.
8. Implement recommendations.
9. Recalibrate benchmarks.

Although many readers might conclude that one could easily deduce the additional four steps of the nine-step model from the five-step version, for the first-time user the nine-step model is often more helpful without being overly burdensome.

An even more rigorous approach is the five-phase, twelve-step version used by leading companies such as benchmark trailblazer the Xerox Corporation:

Phase 1: Planning

1. Identify what to benchmark.
2. Identify comparable companies.
3. Determine data collection method and collect data.

Phase 2: Analysis

4. Determine current performance gap.
5. Project future performance levels.

Phase 3: Integration

6. Communicate findings and gain acceptance.
7. Establish functional goals.

Phase 4: Action

8. Develop action plans.
9. Implement specific actions and monitor progress.
10. Recalibrate benchmarks.

Phase 5: Maturity

11. Attain leadership position.
12. Fully integrate practices into processes.

As with other innovation strategies described in this book, benchmarking has migrated among the private, public, and non-profit sectors, being modified and customized along the way. While substantial differences among the three sectors can profoundly influence the nature and efficacy of a particular innovation strategy (reengineering and privatization, for example), a good benchmarking process, such as those just presented, should work well for almost any organization, regardless of sector, product, or service.

A benchmarking fever began going around governments in the 1990s. With so much experience in so many different settings, a great deal has been learned about what does and does not work in the public sector. The best model designed specifically for the public sector that we have found has the following seven steps:

1. Determine which units or processes will benefit most.
2. Identify key variables to measure cost, quality, and efficiency.
3. Pick the best-in-class for each benchmark.
4. Measure the performance of the best-in-class model chosen.
5. Measure or define the gap between your organization and the best-in-class.
6. Agree on actions to close the gap.
7. Implement the action agenda and monitor your progress.

Each of the four benchmarking models just presented has their ardent supporters who believe they have found the one best way to execute effective benchmarking. We believe that each of the four models is among the best yet developed, and if any one of them fits your organization, we encourage you to use it. For those of you who are still searching for another way, our own generic model follows.

1. *Pick your benchmarking targets carefully.* In our experience, more fatal mistakes are made at the beginning of the benchmarking exercise than in any other step in the process. You might think

this is the easiest part of the exercise because you know your organization and you know what needs to be improved. Probably so, but sometimes all that knowledge can get in the way of success.

Before you realize it, you and your team will have targeted virtually every process and most units in your organization for improvement, establishing a research task substantial enough to sink the entire benchmarking exercise before you even get to the improvement agenda. You need to target a limited number of key areas at the outset. If possible, they should be processes or units that are easily measured and for which you already know there are some outstanding organizations doing what you do, only better.

2. *Identify your performance indicators.* The initial inclination is to better the best in every aspect—quality, quantity, cost, efficiency, speed, and customer satisfaction. Ambitious goals can be useful, particularly if you hope to leapfrog your competition. At the same time, you need to limit your scope to the most important indicators if you are to accomplish the process in a reasonable time frame and at a manageable cost. You need to consider carefully the cost of gathering data, the industry standards for measurement, management's central concerns, customer desires, and the comprehensiveness of the package of indicators selected for benchmarking.

3. *Select your role model.* Picking the appropriate standard of comparison is complicated. By what criteria do you pick your benchmark objective? Should you select a different organization for each measure or should you compare your organization on every measure with some overall best-in-class, based on some composite rating?

Just as important: What is the appropriate standard—the best in the world, the best in the nation, the best in your field, the best in your region, the best of your size, the best in your city, or the best in your organization? And, do you want to compare yourselves with only those in your sector—public, private, or nonprofit—or are you looking to learn from and become the best, regardless of sector? There is no one right answer to any of these questions. It may not always be feasible or affordable to seek to become the best in the world, regardless of sector.

A benchmarking team must inject realism at every step of the improvement process. While ambition is good, time and resources are limited. Also, the wider the team casts its net, the more difficult the comparisons become, and often the more expensive the analysis turns out to be. Out-of-category and out-of-sector comparisons are most likely to identify a creative "out-of-the-box" innovation, but such ideas are also likely to be the most difficult to implement and the most likely to fail. The choice of appropriate role models is a balancing act among resources, realism, and potential gains.

4. *Gauge the gap.* What are your role model organizations doing in the key benchmarked processes that you are not? You will probably need to modify their practices to fit your process, particularly if your role model is of substantially different size, from a different sector, or operates in a very different culture or society. Remember to focus on those activities that will have the greatest potential to yield improvements valued by your customers, consumers, clients, or citizens.

As it is for students, the inclination is always to study and measure what you already know well and to avoid studying what you find hard to learn. In organizations there is often a tendency to focus on internal processes that are easy to measure and change but that have an impact on outcomes that is valued by the customer either minimally or not at all. In gauging the important gaps you must simultaneously develop a plan to close that gap or the entire benchmarking effort is no more than an academic exercise.

5. *Monitor progress.* Once the plan to bridge the performance gap has been implemented, you must continue to measure and monitor your organization's improvement. Here we suggest that you follow the TQM principle that the process of improvement is never finished. You can always do better. Although your initial objective may be to close the performance gap between your organization and your role model, your ultimate objective should be to leapfrog their current performance and become their role model.

Benefits of Benchmarking and Performance Management

Benchmarking is an attractive innovation strategy because it can be relatively easy to understand and apply. It is something that many of us have done, albeit a little less rigorously, without knowing to call it benchmarking. The methodology is flexible and can be modified to fit within a wide range of settings, budgets, and time horizons. It also does not require extensive or expensive training or new equipment to get started. A pen and notepad, flip charts and markers, Post-its, a telephone, a Rolodex, and the key players responsible for the process to be benchmarked are really all you need to get under way.

The benchmarking process has value even if the desired improvements are not achieved. By continuously seeking to identify the best-in-class and to duplicate or surpass their performance, an organization shapes its culture and behavior with a strong spirit of competitiveness, pride, confidence, energy, and a drive to always do better. Benchmarking fosters the formation of teams and teamwork. It encourages a concern for customers, the setting of priorities, and a commitment to measure performance on an ongoing basis (Ammons, 1996).

Benchmarking also fuels out-of-the-box thinking and a constant search for best practices. Indianapolis mayor Stephen Goldsmith won a 1995 Ford Foundation/Kennedy School Innovation Prize for his use of competitively bid, performance-based contracting out of city services while including in the competition city employees, who have been winning a significant number of contracts. Mayor Goldsmith frequently tells those seeking to learn his secrets of success that his best talent is identifying the best in the business for whatever municipal service he is seeking to improve and then getting their permission to copy what they are already doing. Goldsmith's self-assessment is that he is a consummate benchmarker.

In government, organizations are frequently drawn into crisis-precipitated "fire-drill behavior," in which the best and brightest staff members are continuously stampeding from one key problem-solving exercise to the next without any regard for the organization's performance in its key areas of responsibility. Performance measurement reports, established by means of benchmarking, can remind an organization of its service priorities and responsibilities. Crises must still be addressed promptly, but performance measurement and benchmarking help to ensure that organizational resources are properly allocated to meet both long- and short-term goals and responsibilities.

As the U.S. Environmental Protection Agency's (EPA) Region II office shifted from its traditional hierarchical structure to a "reinvented" team structure, its managers struggled with the daunting task of redefining performance measures (or "beans") for the region and job performance measures for the individual to reflect the new organization. Fairly measuring performance and rewarding superior work is difficult in an agency such as the EPA, even in stable times, as it tends to be dominated by the herd response. To find good answers to their questions, Region II benchmarked the other EPA regional offices. The good news: the offices in the Pacific Northwest and New England were working on similar concerns and had developed models that proved useful in Region II.

Benchmarking helps to focus attention on accountability. It can assist in making budget choices and negotiating with the chief executive for additional resources. Benchmarking can keep an organization from being satisfied with "good enough" and focused on being "all that it can be." Benchmarking can also guide a move to contract out or outsource, and then help to evaluate the quality and value of contracted services on a regular basis. At its best, benchmarking can help to establish a practical score card for the organization that keeps it focused on what is important to its customers, its owners, and its evaluators.

Costs of Benchmarking and Performance Management

At its worst, benchmarking can be both too easy and too hard. It is often too easy to identify best-in-the-world comparisons that are not attainable, affordable, or even desirable. Benchmarking is easily misused by higher-ups simply to preordain unreachable targets. This outcome is all too familiar in both the public and private sectors.

In the private sector, AT&T's failed effort to buy its way into the computer business through its purchase of NCR is perhaps an example of overambitious benchmarking. Clothing retailers seem to benchmark against one another continuously, which seems to create an endless cycle of expansion, contraction, bankruptcy, and start-ups. The same phenomenon seems to prevail in the retail home electronics industry.

In government, opponents of welfare reform in the United States argue that supporters erroneously used Wisconsin reform efforts as a benchmark for the new national system. The critics maintain that the benchmark was misused, because the Wisconsin economy is healthier and its population less diverse and problem-plagued than the typical urban state in which most welfare-dependent families reside. Finding appropriate benchmarks for welfare reform is greatly complicated by absence of consensus on the program's goal among U.S. policymakers—Are we trying simply to reduce the welfare rolls? Are we working to eliminate poverty? Or is the central focus to establish a universal work ethic?

The benchmark for successful privatization—Great Britain—has not worked well in many African nations. Lower asset values, much greater needs for operating revenues, and less analytic capacity on the government side of the negotiation has often meant that private buyers have acquired assets at a small fraction of their value in Guinea and Mali, for example.

Benchmarking can become bogged down in measurement and lose sight of the real performance improvement desired, particularly if that outcome is difficult to quantify. It can become very complicated for public organizations with multiple goals and objectives, particularly when both the outcome and the process by which the outcome is achieved are equally important. Measurement can also lead to placing undue importance on what are, in reality, very small differences.

As part of its effort to reform government and do more with less, the City of New York began to produce the Mayor's Management Report in the 1970s. The report summarized the performance of city agencies in achieving a series of service delivery, efficiency, and fiscal management targets. The early reports were about twenty pages long and were enormously helpful to the mayor's office, the budget office, agency commissioners, the press, and the public in beginning to look beyond expenditure control toward expenditure effectiveness. By the early 1990s, the report exceeded two hundred pages, with literally thousands of indicators compared against targets on a quarterly basis. Despite a stellar staff, glossy cover, and ceremonial press conference presided over by the mayor, the enlarged report attracted attention only on the rare occasions when it identified a significant failure of an agency to reach or exceed an important target. Too much measurement either overwhelmed the reader or fueled suspicions that so much success in a city with so many needs and demands was just not likely.

Gathering data may be more difficult than just picking up a telephone. Many times, information on key services is not collected, and often there is not a system in place to begin to do so. Even if the data collection system can be established, the reliability of the data collected is often suspect, particularly if the data are collected by those whose performance will be thereby evaluated. Traffic tickets that cannot be enforced often result from management pressure on traffic enforcement personnel to write more tickets. Police officers make arrests to meet their quota, knowing the case against the individual is weak or nonexistent. Welfare caseworkers are often forced to manage their caseloads with an eye first on federal compliance audits and second on helping the family in need.

Comparability of your data with those collected by your role model may also present serious difficulties. Major differences in size, geography, climate, culture, reporting, and accounting standards are just a few of the factors that impact comparability and that may make meaningful, direct quantitative comparisons impossible. The welfare reform and privatization examples previously discussed illustrate this issue of comparability.

Indicators quickly proliferate, targets escalate, and time requirements explode. Over time the benchmarking process can become so routine or political that the press, elected officials, and the public come to view the indicators as self-serving and without credibility, as became the case with the Mayor's Management Report in New York City.

In the private sector, the "facts" presented are generally perceived as creations of an imaginative advertising executive, with little or no relation to reality. Do you really believe AT&T, MCI, or Sprint's claims about which long distance calling rates are cheaper? Many of AT&T's commercials actually focus in on the industry's overall lack of credibility (honesty) with the consumer—they don't say they are cheaper, they say their rates are easy to understand.

At its worst, benchmarking can be a meaningless, time-consuming, and expensive exercise in data collection and reporting that diverts attention from the real work of the organization. Done poorly or dishonestly, benchmarking can undermine the organization's credibility and reputation. It can discourage creativity by focusing on the innovations of other organizations and thereby prevent breakthrough ideas. Finally, it can put a ceiling on ambition and achievement. As Deming so persuasively argued, a performance target can be the major obstacle to better quality and higher output.

We believe that benchmarking is an essential component of any successful management innovation strategy. It can be effective as a stand-alone, quick-fix, "How are we doin'?" technique. And it has great value as a guide for a strategic planning process, as a method of deciding which process to reengineer, and as a means to learning where privatization and contracting out have been used to the greatest advantage. Benchmarking also fosters teamwork.

The decision to benchmark is simply the decision to be open to learning from the experience of other organizations. It is hard to argue against the idea of learning. The issue for the creative public manager is, Where does benchmarking fit into an innovation strategy? and Which benchmarking method best fits the organization's needs and culture?

Benchmarking seems to increase in effectiveness with practice and experience. Proper planning and goal setting are much more important than data gathering. Implementing an improvement is more important than finding the best possible role model. In short, commitment to the underlying principles of benchmarking can be as valuable to your organization as the benchmarking exercise itself.

Chapter Six

| **Team Management**

Organizations are increasingly turning to team management as an effective strategy to respond to an external environment that is characterized by turmoil and change. Rapid change, technological innovation, competition, and globalization are affecting even community-based organizations with a neighborhood focus. Teams seem to function more effectively than individuals in such an environment.

Teams pool knowledge, experience, skills, and perspectives. They facilitate brainstorming, encourage creativity, and are better able to handle cross-functional assignments. Teams seem to cope better with rapid change, short response times, and uncertainty. They are an important component of Total Quality Management (TQM), and many organizations learn the value of teams as they experiment with TQM. However, the use of teams to accomplish work objectives predates TQM by a wide margin.

The use of teams in a work environment goes back hundreds if not thousands of years. The manager's exhortation to employees to display more team spirit and teamwork is familiar to most people in most cultures, and usually begins in the first few days of their first formal job. Yet only recently has team management emerged as a free-standing, well-developed strategy for the workplace.

Most people first experience the team approach through sports and games, not at work. We think of our own participation in organized games of baseball, soccer, basketball, hockey, or football. Television sports commentators frequently explain the triumph of the apparently less talented team as the result of their superior teamwork, saying, "The whole is greater than the sum of its parts."

It is logical that success in team sports is often closely connected to superior teamwork. How team practices and behaviors can be used to make complex business, government, or nonprofit organizations more successful is less clear. For nearly 150 years, the model for successful work organizations has been the hierarchical bureaucracy—a structure that encourages specialization and subordination. Nevertheless, for decades successful sports managers and coaches have made a respectable second income out of lecturing and writing about how the lessons of the ball field can be effectively applied in the conference and board room.

Groups of individuals often come together for the purpose of accomplishing a task, whether it be charitable, political, or social. Raising funds for the needy during the holiday season, cleaning up a vacant lot in the neighborhood, or organizing a softball league picnic are common group projects that many of us seek to accomplish more efficiently and harmoniously through the use of team-based strategies. But not every group of people is a team, and surely not every team is effective. In our view, teams must be clearly defined, well designed, and properly equipped for the mission they are to accomplish, if they are to be successful.

There is a significant difference between a *work group* and a *work team* (Guzzo and Dickson, 1996). A work group is comprised of individuals who see themselves and are seen by others as a social entity, who are interdependent because of the tasks they perform, and who perform tasks that affect those beyond the group. Work groups are important and have an impact on organizational behavior and performance.

Work teams have a much greater impact on organizations, and far-reaching implications for management and productivity. To us, even the word *team* connotes much more import than the word *group*. Groups evolve into teams when they become self-conscious, when their members share goals and a commitment to the team, and when they endeavor to enhance their functioning (Guzzo and Dickson, 1996). Teams focus on collective work products and performance results (Katzenbach and Smith, 1993).

In a workplace context, a team is a group of people pooling their talents, skills, knowledge, and experience in a mutually supportive effort to complete a project, reach a goal, or solve a problem. A team can also be defined as a group of people drawn from different disciplines who work together on a semipermanent basis to carry out critical organizational tasks. Teams should create synergy, enthusiasm, and support, as well as a spirit of "all for one and one for all."

The team approach should empower decision making at a lower level than might otherwise be the case. A team-based organization facilitates learning among workers and the development of new expertise. Teams are generally seen as one dimension of quality leadership. In our view, an effective team is also characterized by a commitment to a common goal or purpose, a consensus on performance goals and objectives, and a willingness on the part of its members to hold themselves mutually accountable for the team's work (Katzenbach and Smith, 1993).

In modern organizations, teams are rapidly becoming the primary mechanism of innovation and change, capitalizing on leadership and cross-functional teamwork while simultaneously overcoming the bureaucratic ills of subordination and gamesmanship. The team approach can have a dramatic, positive impact on the roles of managers and subordinates, and thereby on the organization as a whole. The team focus can shift an organization from managing by control to managing by commitment. It can change the institution's emphasis from individual motivation and output to team spirit and overall accomplishment; from the traditional focus on organizing, staffing, and evaluating, to coaching and facilitating.

Teams are typically comprised of five to seven members, with one member designated by senior management to serve as the team leader. Teams are often created to complete a specific project or to perform an important ongoing function. The creation of a team is generally an indication from the top that the work of the team is an organizational priority.

Teams are often organized outside the traditional organizational hierarchy but they report to a person in authority who is part of the hierarchy. Team membership includes a responsibility to participate in and contribute to the work of the team. The work of the team becomes the work of the individual, but team members often retain responsibility for individual assignments as well. Teams are usually organized as standing teams, project teams, or crisis teams (Scholtes, 1996). With the increased focus on and interest in team management in the past decade, other specialized team types have developed, including top management teams, process improvement teams (the connection to reengineering should be obvious), and self-managed teams.

Standing teams. Certain projects, types of projects, issues, or customer demands frequently recur within an organization. Standing teams can deal with issues that recur seasonally, with a large or important client or customer, or with a problem for which the combined specialties of several individuals is required. A standing team could be used to respond to legislative inquiries, to comment on proposed new regulations, to assess new technologies, to serve as a quality council, to open a city's swimming pools each summer, or to plan and coordinate opening week of the school year. Unlike a project team, standing teams have a life beyond any one project and could be viewed as a semipermanent part of the organization.

Project teams. As the name implies, some teams are assembled to accomplish a distinct and particular task. Project teams are probably the most common and familiar use of teams; the approach has been characteristic of large engineering and management consulting firms for decades. In this methodology, the appropriate mix of specialists from across the permanent organization are brought together to complete an important assignment with clearly defined goals and deadlines. The team members retain their organizational home base and their location in the hierarchy but are now jointly accountable to their permanent supervisor and the project team leader.

Once the project is accomplished, the team members either return to their organizational home base or join another team directed at a different set of objectives. A typical project for such a team might be the installation of a new computer system, the relocation of the office, or the staffing of a new organizational responsibility. The project characteristics that commonly dictate the need to create a project team include importance, complexity, time sensitivity, cross-functionality, and multidisciplinarity. Construction projects readily come to mind when thinking about project teams.

Crisis teams. The nature of a crisis team is obvious from its name. Government organizations often rock from side to side as a herd of staffers run from crisis to crisis as they are identified by the commissioner, the mayor, the governor, the president, or the press.

Private and nonprofit organizations are usually less volatile or responsive, but they too can be thrown into chaos by external events, such as the Exxon Valdez disaster, the chemical explosion at Bhopal, fiscal improprieties at the United Way, or media focus on children killed by automobile air bag "safety devices."

Crisis teams can be used to mitigate the constant disruption of the organization's regular work (which can evolve into a crisis if it doesn't get done). Crisis teams can be organized as project teams; a new team of experts can be assembled to deal with each new crisis as it arises. Or they can be structured similarly to a standing team, as a swat team of talented individuals who work particularly well in a highly charged, dangerous environment. Generally, the work of crisis teams is very high profile, and selection for participation should be accorded the appropriate organizational prestige and recognition.

Top management teams. Top management teams establish the central mission of an organization. They are responsible for setting the strategy that enables the organization to reach its desired goals. They also set the tone and the strategy for the organization.

Teams are not the answer to every organizational problem, nor are they necessarily the best way to accomplish every organizational objective. At the same time, as top management teams seek to improve their organization's performance, they frequently discover that the team structure can help them meet their goals (Katzenbach and Smith, 1993).

Process improvement teams. Process improvement teams are designed to enhance an organization's service delivery performance or the economy and efficiency of its operation. Process improvement teams are closely associated with TQM, and now with reengineering as well. Process improvement teams are generally focused on meeting and exceeding the needs and desires of external customers. To do this, they seek to answer such questions as, Who are the customers of the process and what expectations do they hold? Who are the suppliers of the process? How does the work flow within the process? How is quality measured and what are the quality indicators? What are the causes of flaws in the process (Koehler and Panowski, 1996, p. 37)? Process improvement teams use TQM techniques such as brainstorming, fishboning, and flowcharting to help answer these questions. Because process improvement teams are generally grounded in TQM, they seek to improve the work process continually. These teams therefore are often in place for a longer time than a project or crisis team, although their membership may change over time.

Self-managed teams. Self-managed teams are authorized to modify the processes they oversee as needed to achieve desired outcomes. The team accepts the responsibility for controlling and improving the work process they manage, and in return they are given substantial discretion to modify procedures to ensure that the work gets done. The team is evaluated by its success in achieving the desired process results. Self-managed teams control work schedules, work assignments, work flows, budget, maintenance, and problem solving.

Self-managed teams are not required to seek approval from management or even to inform management immediately of decisions they make concerning process improvement. Although this sort of latitude is common in the private sector, public sector organizations are seldom willing or able to give line personnel this degree of discretion. The intrinsic checks and balances of a democratic public sector makes such unilateral decision making by non-elected civil servants unacceptable.

How Teams Work

The recent flurry of articles, books, and instructional videos on team management can create the impression that teams are a recent insight and innovation. In fact, behavioral scientists and management experts have been studying and using team-based improvement strategies for more than a half century. Most students of management have encountered the landmark research of Elton Mayo on the functions of teams and informal work groups at Western Electric's Hawthorne factory near Chicago. Mayo and his researchers experimented with the impact of environmental change on work group productivity.

In their first experiments on workplace lighting, Mayo and his team found that productivity increased for both the experimental and control groups. Over the next few years, the Mayo group introduced a variety of changes into the work environment to measure the impact on productivity and morale. At least ten different changes were tried, each accompanied by extensive communication between the test group and the researchers. Output increased with each change in the environment (Pugh and Hickson, 1989).

Over time it became clear to the researchers that the experimental group had become what we now call a work team. They had developed a clear goal, a system of communication and participation, and a decision-making structure. They also had developed a sophisticated relationship to the researchers. The group had not just evolved into a team; it had become an effective team (Parker, 1996).

The control in Mayo's workplace experiments involved simply observing a work group without making any changes in their environment or engaging in extensive communication with that group. What the Mayo researchers found was that in an unstructured environment the control group established its own performance criteria for individuals and used peer pressure to enforce it. The result was lower overall productivity. The group became what we would now call an ineffective team (Parker, 1996).

Following Mayo, a number of noted social scientists, including Kurt Lewin, Douglas McGregor, Rensis Likert, and Chris Argris studied teams as an organizational strategy to accomplish work (Parker, 1996, pp. 18–40). Their research is extremely helpful in discovering the behaviors and procedures that contribute to making teams effective and ineffective. Among the factors found to contribute to effective team performance are clear purpose, informality, participation, listening, respectful debate, consensus decision making, open and continuous communication, clear roles and assignments, shared leadership, diversity, and a capacity for self-assessment. Among the factors that characterize ineffective teams are unclear mission; formal, tense communication; much talk, little action; intense, private disagreement; hierarchical decision making; distrust; confused roles; and no self-assessment (Parker, 1996).

Team management took a major step forward as a management strategy with the emergence of the TQM movement, led by W. Edwards Deming. Deming put the team-based organization at the center of his Fourteen Points (Walton, 1986, pp. 34–36). He urged managers to break down staff areas so that employees could work as a team to solve or foresee problems (point 9). He viewed teams as a way to get away from mass inspections and instead enlist workers in an organization improvement process (point 3). And Deming argued that teams could replace ineffective slogans and targets imposed by management with their own spirit and self-generated commitment to improvement (point 10).

Deming believed that teamwork is essential to sustained organizational success, but the team approach is not nurtured by nor does it take root readily in the typical hierarchical design. Most organizations foster commitment to limited departmental goals. When departmental goals are in conflict (as they often are), the organization inhibits and limits its own potential. Deming thought that teamwork could mitigate this self-destructive behavior.

The team approach comes to many organizations as part of a TQM initiative. Teams are essential to the success of TQM. However, team management is also possible as a stand-alone strategy, and that approach has become increasingly popular. As the critics of TQM have become louder and more numerous, it is less fashionable for top management to introduce TQM. Team management is still relatively new and can bring with it many of the benefits of TQM without some of the negative baggage.

While there is now a growing body of literature on team management as a stand-alone strategy, most of the literature consists of case studies (the best sources available include Peters, 1992; Katzenbach and Smith, 1993; Appelbaum and Batt, 1987; Parker, 1996). In addition, good information is available on what can go wrong and how to correct the problem. What's missing is a simple step-by-step guide for getting started.

On the basis of our work with numerous organizations trying to bring teams into their structure, we developed the eight-step strategy presented in Exhibit 6.1. Bringing the team approach to an organization begins with creating an environment that is conducive to their growth.

1. *Create a team culture.* According to many popular management experts, teams are essential to organizational success in our modern, rapidly changing, technologically complex world. Many innovative companies, such as Motorola, Kodak, 3M, and McKinsey use teams as their basic work units. These companies rely on the team structure to disseminate important information more effectively throughout their organization, to facilitate problem

Exhibit 6.1. Guide to Making Team Management Work.

1. Create a team culture.
2. Integrate teams into the organization structure.
3. Reward team participation.
4. Establish clear rules for team operation.
5. Recruit team leaders and members.
6. Develop a team identity.
7. Provide the tools and track progress.
8. Recognize team accomplishments and conclude or redirect the team.

solving, to accomplish cross-functional projects, to connect the formal and informal organization structures, to simplify work processes, and to teach employees to work together.

For teams to be successful, it must be clear to the entire organization that the teams were created by top management to deal with projects, issues, and crises of the highest priority. Teams should be created to deal only with real issues, and they should be disbanded or reorganized when their original objective is achieved or disappears.

Teams should report to a high-level decision maker in the organization. Assignment to a team should be characterized by top management as a career boost, and a competitive process to select team members can reinforce the importance of teams.

2. *Integrate teams into the organization structure.* Teams must become part of the regular organization structure. Just as with successful TQM initiatives, there must not be a clear distinction between "teamwork" and "regular work." Otherwise, the work of the team and its members will become marginalized.

Teams should report directly to a manager who has supervisory authority in the traditional organization's chain of command. Some teams will require the full-time effort of its members; others may not. A dual reporting structure, similar to that of matrix organizations, may make sense when the work of teams requires less than full-time involvement. The time commitment should be made explicit in the charge that authorizes the team.

For the most part, teams are formed within the existing formal organizational units and are established by the unit's manager, who acts with the authority of top management. Where teams cut across organizational boundaries, they must be established cooperatively by the managers of all the units involved. These cross-cutting teams generally report to one manager.

3. *Reward team participation.* Teams and team members should be evaluated in the same way, using the same yardstick that applies to the regular organizational units. Evaluation should be routinized but kept short and simple. The evaluation should assess the extent to which the team accomplished its mission and the contribution of each member to the team's achievements. Bonus payments, compensation, promotions, and recognition must be connected directly to the team evaluation system, just as with the standard evaluation process.

Teamwork should be incorporated into formal position descriptions and salary classification systems. In some organizations, this may also require the creation of alternative career path options, enabling employees to move up, earn more money, and enhance their organizational prestige by working in teams, instead of climbing the traditional organizational hierarchy. If the team innovation is to succeed, the salary trends and reputation of those working predominantly in teams must at least keep pace with those of their peers who have chosen the more established management career path.

4. *Establish clear rules for team operation.* Clear ground rules are essential to team management. Team members must understand what work they are to accomplish, why the team approach was chosen to accomplish it, what their ultimate objective is, and what improvements are expected. They also need to know the schedule, including estimated beginning and end dates.

Important questions must be anticipated and answered up front. What resources will be available to assist the team? What training will occur? What internal and external support will be put behind the team initiative?

The team leader should prepare formal agendas in advance for all team meetings, and those agendas should be retained as an ongoing record of the team's operation. Someone, usually the team leader, should serve as the facilitator of team meetings. On a rotating basis, team members should keep minutes to record team activities and accomplishments.

There should be a formal structure and schedule for teams to report their progress to the regular organizational hierarchy. Team leaders, occasionally joined by some team members, should have periodic, face-to-face meetings with senior management. And there should be formal, written feedback from management to the team on their activities and to evaluate their performance.

5. *Recruit team leaders and members.* If at all possible, recruitment of team leaders and members should be on a competitive basis, enabling management to attract the organization's best and brightest to high-priority assignments. Management should select a mix of skills, knowledge, and complementary personalities. And management must reinforce its commitment to team assignments as career makers.

Leadership and facilitation skills are clearly essential for the effective team leader. The ability to work well in a less structured environment is an important attribute for both team leaders and team members. Self-starters are obvious choices for team assignments, as are people who have a track record of working well with others. While self-selection for team assignments is preferable, it may be necessary for management to assign particular individuals to teams, especially to achieve the proper mixture of talents and knowledge.

The team leader is the manager of the team's work. He or she schedules, organizes, and facilitates team meetings, ensures that the assignment is fully understood by all members, facilitates group communication, and helps address and resolve group conflicts. With input from the members, the leader develops the team's work plan, keeps the team on schedule, and maintains team records and files. Management need not select the most senior member of the team as leader. In fact, communication may be facilitated if the highest ranking member is not chosen as leader. A good team leader does not dictate to the team or try to boss them around. Rather, the effective team leader involves and engages team members in the group's deliberations and decision-making process.

The team leader should never try to do all of the team's work single-handedly. A good team leader assigns manageable tasks to each team member. The leader is also a team member and should therefore be assigned nonmanagement work, just like every other member of the team.

Team members need to recognize that the work of the team is now part of their regular job—in some cases, their only job. This is not extra work but rather a priority assignment from top management. Team members are expected to participate actively in group meetings and to contribute their expertise to the team's work, including helping to collect data on current levels of performance.

6. *Develop a team identity.* Every team is a complicated entity. Members need to work out their individual and group identities and roles, how to communicate effectively, how the team experience intersects with their career goals, and how to work well in a less structured environment. Every team will have its own unique personality. Most teams can work well, but some will do so more quickly and with less effort than others.

One important key to team success is knowing what to expect. To prepare participants for a team experience, clear communication of expectations and training is essential. Knowledgeable outside consultants can be helpful, particularly in the early stages of team management. There are also handbooks and videotapes available that in-house facilitators can use to get teams off on the right foot. In our view, there is no better team management resource than the second edition of *The Team Handbook,* by Peter Scholtes and his colleagues (1996).

As teams are formed and begin operation, they will likely wrestle with and benefit from outside assistance in addressing the following questions: How does each member fit into this new group? Will the team member be viewed as an insider or outsider? Will he or she be accepted or have trouble fitting in? How will decisions be made? Will the team be influential or ignored? How well will this team work together? Teams will progress and evolve. The road to effective team performance will not always be smooth. Help from outside the team and outside the organization can enable the team to reach its full potential.

7. *Provide the tools and track progress.* Teams can conduct analytic work, supervise contracts, coordinate work production, or manage any responsibility or initiative that could be handled by a traditional organizational unit. While a new team may take a certain

amount of time to organize and achieve its peak performance level, once it is up and running it can achieve a great deal in a short amount of time. Unlike regular organizational units, teams are sometimes exempted from normal organizational duties, such as budget-making exercises and personnel processing and evaluation reports.

Ongoing support and direction from top management is essential. Some teams also need technical assistance from outside experts. An internal coach can serve as the point person for all teams and as a symbol of the organization's commitment to the initiative. Training throughout the transition to a team-based organization is also key.

Teams need to be given the time and facilities to do their work. Clear roles and responsibilities will ensure that the time provided is used effectively. Timed agendas, minutes, and an updated work plan will help keep the team on schedule and top management informed and up-to-date on their progress. The consultant and organization coach must help the team leader to encourage cooperative team behaviors and balanced participation, and to face conflict, treating it as a group problem as often as possible.

8. *Recognize team accomplishments and conclude or redirect the team.* Many organizations do not pay sufficient attention to properly ending teams. For team management to prosper in an organization, participants must sense the importance of the effort, and nonparticipants must be motivated to "get in the game." Care must be taken to give each team an appropriate, informative, and inspired kickoff, but it is equally important that teams end well.

A team should end when the task it was organized to accomplish is completed, when the crisis it was created to deal with has passed, or when the ongoing assignment it was to handle ceases to be an organizational priority. Management should make every effort, if warranted, to praise the team and its performance widely, and to provide suitable roles for reassigned team members.

The team approach offers top management flexibility, provides employees with new challenges and variety, and helps to create an agile and learning organization that can thrive in a competitive and rapidly changing environment. To use teams to their maximum advantage, management must end teams as frequently, and with as much fanfare, as it begins them.

Benefits of Team Management

A team approach to work has been common in many cultures for hundreds if not thousands of years. Since 1990, large multinational corporations have been using teams to accomplish an ever-larger percentage of their work. The team approach is prominent and credited with a large measure of the success of leading corporations such as Motorola, Ford, and General Electric (Katzenbach and Smith, 1993).

More recently, governments and nonprofit organizations have achieved significant improvements in their performance through the use of team management. The U.S. Environmental Protection Agency (EPA) chose team management as the best method of meeting the Clinton administration's National Performance Review directives for less hierarchy, greater focus on customers, and empowerment of employees. EPA is also using cross-functional teams to communicate to those it regulates, as well as to customers, more clearly and consistently; to save resources by reducing duplication; and to make decisions more quickly. Teams can perform well because they bring together people with complementary skills and experiences that collectively exceed the capacity of any one of the members or of the members working together but independently. The broad base of teams enables them to respond well to a wide variety of challenges from customers, to a changing environment, and to technological innovation.

In Virginia, Arlington County manager Tony Gander used a mixed team of managers and workers to create a vision statement and set of principles to guide his efforts to improve county services in a tight budget environment. Armed with six principles—high-quality service, commitment to employees, diversity, empowerment, improvement, teamwork, and leadership—the governmentwide implementation team has helped departments to improve services to the public and to deal more effectively with emergencies. The team's successes range from overcoming a water contamination crisis without requiring local residents to boil their water, to picking up the autumn leaves a month faster than the regular timetable (Parkhurst, 1994).

The communication skills and networks that successful teams develop enable them to respond quickly and flexibly to new problems and a changing environment. Individuals seldom have sufficient time, skills, and attitude to overcome new obstacles as rapidly or effectively as teams. In Washington State, for example, design teams in the State Department of Licensing sped up the processing of a wide variety of filing and application procedures, saving their customers time, aggravation, and money. Extensive cross-training enabled Washington's employees to understand each other's work, reducing office segmentation and empowering employees to perform a wider variety of tasks. Among other achievements, the team converted the complicated and labor-intensive Uniform Commercial Code Process into a one-stop procedure, earning them the 1994 Governor's Award for Outstanding Public Service. A second team in the department was able to streamline and automate the disabled parking permit application process, reducing it from thirty days down to forty-eight hours (Rodkey, 1994).

Teams also facilitate the breaking down of barriers between specializations, genders, age groups, races, ethnic groups, and communities. With such barriers reduced, an environment of greater trust and mutual confidence develops, as well as a stronger commitment to organizational goals. At the City University of New York's Brooklyn College, President Vernon Lattin directed one of his top deputies, Ella Friedman Weiss, to embark on a multiyear strategy to make teamwork (TQM) "just the way we work around here." Although the effort continues to grow at the college, teams have already helped to bridge not only genders, age, races, ethnicity, and neighborhoods, but also the historical antipathy among and between college administrators, faculty, support personnel, and students. The results to date include more timely and accurate graduation lists, expedited adjunct faculty hiring and timely paychecks once they are teaching, easier access to funds for student clubs and activities, and a more responsive facility maintenance and repair operation. Long-standing class divisions and biases have been overcome, enabling major improvements to occur without additional staff or equipment (Amos, Cohen, and Eimicke, 1996).

New beneficial behaviors have developed as well. Faculty members take minutes at team meetings. A clerical employee took interest in and exhibited a flair for flowcharting and systems analysis and with the help and support of other members of her team enrolled in the college to pursue a bachelor's degree. The entire community has begun to accept personal responsibility for the buildings and grounds, resulting in a much more effective maintenance program.

Finally, the team approach can make work more fun. Fun at work is important. It can help offset the frequent bad news of downsizings, tight budgets, and escalating global competition. This kind of fun comes out of a shared commitment to meet and work together to overcome organizational problems or accomplish organizational goals. Teams work long, hard, and well because the members enjoy the process of collaboration and achievement. They often celebrate their successes and analyze their failures together, which reinforces the social and positive work aspects of the team experience. There is also the inspirational phenomenon of feeling a part of something greater than oneself (Katzenbach and Smith, 1993).

The New York City Department of Parks and Recreation used TQM's team approach to maintain and improve the most extensive municipal parks system in the world during four years of massive budget cuts and a one-third reduction in full-time staff, from 1991 to 1994. Teams renewed their energy and commitment with picnics, softball games, award ceremonies, and breakfasts. Parks Commissioner Betsy Gotbaum facilitated the fun with logo watch awards, recognition visits to the commissioner's office in Central Park's historic and beautiful Arsenal building, and surprise drop-ins at team meetings. Agency morale remained high and union relations positive throughout Gotbaum's four-year tenure because of her extraordinary talent, hard work, and effective use of teams (Cohen and Eimicke, 1994a).

Costs of Team Management

Parks Commissioner Gotbaum made it clear that teams were the foundation of her management philosophy, but other CEOs often announce implementation of a new team management initiative without conviction or sustained support. Perhaps they read an article in *Business Week* about team management being all the rage among the top companies, or perhaps they picked up a book on the subject while delayed in an airport. In government, the strategy may be imposed by an elected or appointed official seeking to counteract negative publicity or demonstrate a clear break from the previous administration.

Whatever the wrong reason for the announced new initiative, organizational grapevines are quick and effective at spreading the word that this "flavor of the month" management reform is not serious business. This response reinforces the prevailing wisdom that individual performance is the only thing that counts when it comes time for management to consider raises and promotions. Work in teams is soon characterized among workers as a waste of time, as talking and meeting when real work could be getting done on one's own. In such circumstances, the team initiative will almost definitely fail.

At the EPA's Region II headquarters, a high-level, cross-functional team was created to bring team management to their organization, beginning in 1994. The planning team had the support and confidence of the regional administrator. Vice President Al Gore's National Performance Review recommended team management to help flatten hierarchies in federal agencies, to empower federal employees, and to help make agencies more customer service oriented. EPA Administrator Carol Browner embraced the team approach, encouraged its adoption throughout the EPA (including in the regional offices), provided technical assistance, and promised to cut steps in the budget process, reduce personnel red tape, and avoid the bean-counting mentality that could easily doom the new philosophy.

Unfortunately, despite an excellent plan and two years of hard work by the Region II planning team, negative signals from the region's own personnel division undermined the credibility and impaired the effectiveness of the effort. Longtime bureaucrats sent out strong informal signals and messages that the team approach was the pipe dream of the Clinton-Gore administration and would never be integrated into the agency's reward system and career ladders. With the Republican congressional landslide in fall 1994, the administrator approaching four full years in office, and the president's prospects not looking all that good throughout 1995, the team approach was effectively stalemated.

Once President Clinton was reelected, team management supporters had renewed strength and authority. Teams are now operating in Region II, eliminating an entire layer of management. Morale and productivity are up thus far, but it remains unclear whether alternative career paths and reward systems will be created to sustain the team approach over the long haul at EPA.

Except for team sports, most formative experiences in school and social organizations reinforce the importance of individual work and evaluation. It is hardly surprising then that many of us feel uncomfortable and at risk when team management is introduced into the workplace. The problem becomes extreme when the performance evaluation system confirms the prevailing wisdom that individual performance is the only thing that counts when raises and promotions are determined. In such circumstances, expending time and energy in team meetings is at best a waste of time and at worst could even damage one's prospects for a future in management. In the EPA's Region II, when the individual performance appraisal and unit production bean-counting systems did not change, employees heard the message that work in teams did not really count.

Unions are sometimes strongly opposed to team management. They fear that it creates direct communication between top management and line workers on issues that they see as their expertise and responsibility. At the Loretto nonprofit senior housing and health complex in Syracuse, New York, President Jim Introne asked us to serve as consultants as he tried to introduce team management and TQM into his organization in the early 1990s; he turned to these strategies to cope with the fiscal pressures of managed care and Medicaid cutbacks, particularly for residential health care facilities. Fearing that management would develop a direct relationship with line workers and begin to explore new reward and incentives mechanisms outside traditional, confrontational collective bargaining negotiations, his unions struck the facility. Ultimately Introne was forced to abandon his plans for both team management and TQM, despite the enthusiasm of many managers and workers through his organizations.

Parks Commissioner Gotbaum faced the same type of union opposition to her team management approach but was able to overcome it. Her success was in part due to the sheer strength of her personality and her doggedness, and in part due to the dire straits of her agency. In the end the unions felt they had little else to lose by cooperating, and maybe some chance of turning the tide of layoffs and cutbacks.

Teams inevitably face interpersonal conflicts and other obstacles that, if not overcome, can waste the organization's resources, hamper morale, and ultimately snowball into the organization's demise. To prepare individuals for effective team performance, initial training and ongoing access to help and advice are critical. Whether internal or hired consultants are used for training, the organization must carry the expense. In government, training funds are particularly difficult to access, given what now seems to be a continual state of tight budgets.

It is even more expensive but just as important to revise the organization's evaluation and compensation systems to reflect and reward performance in team settings. Career ladders must be created to make sure that talented employees do not come to view team assignments as a career dead end. There must be clear guidelines regarding next assignments when a team completes its work and is disbanded.

During 1996, the welfare-to-work job placement company America Works decided that team management could help its employees achieve an even higher level of job placements and retentions. A detailed discussion of the benefits and challenges of this teams initiative is provided in Chapter Ten of this book.

Finally, moving to team management may require reorganization and therefore is accompanied by the dislocation and expense that come with more traditional restructurings. Job descriptions, career ladders, evaluation systems, and often office configurations will need to be revised. Finally, there is always the danger that the performance improvements anticipated by management will not meet expectations and yet another reorganization will follow.

In many respects, if you are committed to innovate in management, you probably will introduce at least some form of team management into your organization, whether or not you intend to do so. We make the case that without strategic planning as the first step in your innovation plan, you are in grave danger of innovating to get to the wrong result more quickly. Without a team management strategy, your efforts to use reengineering, total quality management, and strategic planning will probably fail. To privatize or contract out successfully, the team approach is certainly very helpful, if not essential. Benchmarking can be done without it, but to what ultimate purpose?

The nature of most work, leaner and flatter organizations, a more educated workforce, more demanding customers, and global competition all suggest team management as a way to enhance organizational performance. In addition, team management is relatively easy to learn about and use. It also works well with other management strategies. And while there are costs and risks, team management is a low-cost, low-tech, and potentially high-return innovation strategy.

| **Privatization**

Definitions of privatization cover a spectrum. Calvin Kent (1987, p. 4) asserts that privatization is "the transfer of functions previously performed exclusively by government, usually at zero or below full-cost prices, to the private sector at prices that clear the market and reflect the full cost of production." Cliff Atherton and Duane Windsor (1987, p. 93) define privatization as "any steps that move away from exclusively public ownership and operation of services or infrastructure." We consider privatization the utilization of private or nongovernmental organizations in the implementation of public policy, often replacing direct government provision of particular programs or services.

As Donald Kettl points out in *Sharing Power: Public Governance and Private Markets* (1993), the privatization of government functions in the United States can be traced to the Revolutionary War. He notes that General Washington often complained about inadequate, shoddy, privately produced uniforms and munitions. Other government functions that were contracted out early in our nation's history were the collection of customs duties from incoming ocean vessels, the operation of the original Secret Service, and the jailing of federal prisoners. Kettl also discusses President Franklin Delano Roosevelt's decision to forge a partnership with the private sector to rapidly build the United States's military capacity during World War II. From a historical perspective, then, privatization is simply a new term for the old practice of contracting out.

Since World War II, the U.S. government has taken a more proactive role in privatization and has forged partnerships with private sector organizations in public policy realms ranging from health care policy to savings and loan bailouts (Kettl, 1993). More recently, both political ideology concerning the proper role and size of government and public sector resource constraints have been the impetus for increased interest in privatization as a public sector management tool (Atherton and Windsor, 1987). President Ronald Reagan embraced privatization after taking cues from governors and mayors throughout the United States where governments had undertaken major privatization efforts. The dismantling of command-and-control economies in the Eastern Bloc countries influenced privatization trends as well (Newland, 1996). The ideological stance that the private sector is more effective than government at performing certain functions coupled with the enduring antitax sentiment of the American people has made privatization a highly popular tool for public managers in recent years.

Politics is of course an inescapable part of the privatization decision. Public sector advocates such as government worker unions argue against contracting out. Conservative politicians argue for maximum feasible privatization. In the mid-1990s privatization was very much in vogue as a cutting-edge technique of public management innovation. With government less popular than ever, and with public funds being stretched over a larger number of competing priorities, elected officials have sought to win popularity by advocating privatization.

In addition, "a more educated and skeptical citizenry . . . is leading many local officials to embrace a new management paradigm and focus their attention on accountability" (Cigler, 1996, 65). Privatization is one means to do so. In the United States, where we have access to a wide and increasing variety of competing brand names and service providers in private markets, citizens are less apt to settle for one choice in public service—direct provision by an agency of government. Elected and appointed public officials alike are implementing privatization schemes as a means to please their constituency and garner public support. Because public and political support are major determinants of a public agency's budget allocation, this is an important issue for public managers.

At the same time, when considering privatization, government officials must remain aware of the often capricious nature of

public opinion. A decision to privatize that was extremely popular
at one time may become the target of criticism if service delivery
is poor or public opinion about the role of government or privatization changes. The violent protest in 1997 against Argentina's successful privatization program provides a good example of this
danger. Privatization brought about a more efficient economy and
a leaner government operation, but it was also accompanied by
layoffs and persistently high unemployment. Balancing the politics
of privatization decisions is therefore a significant challenge for
public decision makers, and adds to the complexity of the privatization decision.

Out of the historical and political environments in which privatization originated, three distinct streams of privatization theory
have emerged. The first stream holds that the private sector is superior to the public sector. Some of privatization's political advocates
argue that private organizations tend to be more efficient than government organizations due to the influence of the profit motive
and the bottom line. In this view, the more that private organizations are involved in the delivery of government services, the more
efficient and cost-effective those services tend to be. E. S. Savas
(1982), an early privatization analyst, holds that government historically has had an "overly dominant role" in providing goods and
services; he advocates a "more limited, modest, sensible role for
government" in the provision of many services (pp. 29, 111). Both
the efficiency and operational elements of Savas's viewpoint rank
private sector service provision above public sector provision
"unless, from an efficiency standpoint, private provision is
markedly inferior to provision by a government entity" (p. 94).

A second approach to privatization was put forward by Savas
(1987) and Osborne and Gaebler (1992) and later termed by Kettl
the competition prescription (1993, p. 1). According to this view, the
key factor that inspires efficiency is not the sector in which an organization operates, but whether or not it must compete for market
share, functions, and resources. From this perspective, the problem of organizational waste occurs in both sectors and stems from
habits born of monopoly. In the private sector, examples of wasteful and inefficient operations include General Motors before Toy-
ota and Honda, AT&T before deregulation, and IBM before

Apple, Microsoft, and the clones. In the public sector, the Defense Department is sometimes seen as a collection of noncompetitive, wasteful organizations. Kettl (1993), as well as other advocates of the competition prescription, believes that the fix for government "is to replace the government's monopoly with the discipline of vigorous competition" (p. 2). The introduction of competition into government service delivery should lead to greater efficiency, force public monopolies to respond to customer preferences, reward innovation where monopoly stifles it, and boost the pride and morale of public employees (Osborne and Gaebler, 1992).

The third stream in privatization theory, and the one we support, is what might be termed *functional matching*. According to this notion, certain functions are most effectively and efficiently performed by the private sector, some by the nonprofit sector, and others by government. For example, police functions are properly governmental, nursing care is often best delivered by nonprofits, and private sector firms often excel in construction and other manufacturing functions. In the case of police functions, for example, the exercise of police authority might result in the loss of an individual's life or liberty. This requires a high level of clearly assignable accountability and therefore should be implemented directly by government. Nursing care, conversely, requires personnel motivated by high levels of compassion rather than by the profit motive. Nonprofits have a particular expertise in recruiting such individuals and infusing them with a strong sense of mission. Finally, manufacturing is best performed by competing, profit-seeking organizations. There is no particular sensitivity, such as individual liberty or the need for compassion, that must be taken into account during the production process.

With a functional matching approach to privatization, organizations involved in formulating and implementing public policy must make the classic business organization make-or-buy decision: Should we do this ourselves or should we buy it from someone else? The answer to this question should be a matter of an organization's strategic analysis of itself, its mission, and its environment, and it should depend on sound analysis of the financial impacts of privatization for the service or product in question. The decision should be particular to the individual management challenge and if at all possible should not be influenced by ideology or other biases. In this stream of thought, privatization should not be applied across the board to governmental functions, but rather should be utilized in the specific instances where the benefits of privatization outweigh its potential disadvantages. Savas believes that "the issue of which [service provision arrangement] is best should properly be addressed as an empirical question, not an ideological or emotional one" (1982, p. 92). It follows, then, that if we consider government provision as part of the opportunity set of service provision arrangements, we must not consider the privatization of government services on purely ideological grounds.

How Privatization Works

Privatization takes four different forms. The first is *contracting out functions that government agencies used to implement with their own staff.* In this form of privatization, government retains management control as well as the option to end a contract and resume direct government control of product or service provision. This is perhaps the most pervasive and widely accepted form of privatization. Governments around the globe have used this technique for hundreds of years.

Among the most common government contracts with private firms are those that are used by agencies to acquire the materials they need to do their work. Governments generally buy through contract rather than make their own weapons, office supplies, computers, cleaning products, vehicles, and so on. Recently governments have begun to contract out the provision of services previously carried out by government workers. Activities in this category include policy analysis, housing management, caring for the homeless, monitoring foster care placements, and job training and placement. Contracts are usually awarded through a competitive Request for Proposal process that judges bids on the basis of price, quality, and other factors.

The second form of privatization involves *turning over a government-run enterprise, such as a telephone system, to the private sector by selling government assets and monopolies to private firms.* The recent trend against socialism, or social ownership of production, has resulted in a massive sell-off of government-owned firms to the private sector, particularly in Western Europe, Latin America, and former Eastern Bloc countries. In many parts of the world, this form of privatization is in fact the main meaning or definition associated with the term *privatization*. In large measure this trend began in the United Kingdom with the election of Margaret Thatcher as prime minister. Thatcherism resulted in $7 billion in state asset sales by 1985 and more than $250 billion by 1991 (Newland, 1996, p. 23). British Air, the national gas utility, and most of British Telecom, as well as scores of other state-run enterprises, were divested. A number of Latin American nations, most notably Argentina and Peru, have seen similar efforts to sell off government companies.

In Germany, reunification resulted in the creation of the Treuhandanstalt, a state-run organization established to broker deals to privatize more than eight thousand industrial firms and twenty thousand small businesses. Despite the mixed reviews it received due to massive levels of unemployment, debt, and alleged investor fraud, by the time the Treuhandanstalt officially closed its doors at the end of 1994 it had injected at least 270 million deutsche marks ($170 billion) into eastern Germany and had successfully converted a command-and-control economy into a private marketplace (Protzman, 1994). Much of the former Soviet Union and its Eastern Bloc have gone through similar periods of asset divestment.

The third form of privatization is a *public-private partnership, in which government and the private sector work jointly, with clearly defined roles, on a public purpose.* New York City's Business Improvement Districts (BIDs) are an example of such a partnership. Under this model, the businesses located within a specific geographic area, such as Times Square, vote to create an organization to provide additional services, such as security, cleanup, maintenance, and marketing, and in return agree to levy a tax assessment on themselves. The city collects these fees as part of the normal taxation process and returns the fees to the BID organization. The BID organization hires staff, buys equipment, and directly provides services traditionally provided by government. Recently some of the larger BIDs have even begun capital projects, funded by a self-imposed tax increment.

The fourth form of privatization involves *public policy that is designed to encourage specific private sector behavior.* It often involves leveraging public resources to encourage private activity. Typical mechanisms include targeted tax credits or deductions, or deregulation. A particularly effective example of this approach is a New York City tax relief program designed to enhance the city's housing stock. The J-51 Tax Exemption and Abatement Program and Section 421a of the New York State Real Property Tax Law are tax incentives designed to preserve and enhance the supply of affordable housing in New York City. By forgoing property taxes, the city encourages private sector landlords and contractors to undertake development and renovation of low-income housing units. This leveraging ensures the provision of needed low-income housing units without requiring the city to build and operate the units. According to the *New York Times* (Hevesi, 1997), nearly 700,000 apartment units received 421a or J-51 benefits in 1996. Together the programs account for approximately $2.2 billion in forgone tax revenue, but government officials, citing the spin-off effects of the tax incentives, believe that the program's benefits are worth it: "A new project provides employment opportunities to the construction industry; that's a plus. The taxes derived from the sale of goods and services in putting the project together, that's a plus. And the physical improvement to a community is also a plus" (Councilman Archie Spigner, quoted in Hevesi, 1997, p. 6).

In another application of this approach, poor neighborhoods can secure industrial investment through the use of government-backed bonds, reducing the cost of capital through lower interest rates and the possibility of tax-free dividends for bondholders. Government can then provide tax advantages to influence the hiring practices of the firm that locates in the new facility. This set of policies provides a privatized version of a government jobs program. It uses public resources and powers to influence private behavior in a way that uses the profit motive to promote social goals. Federal home mortgage insurance and subsidized flood insurance are additional examples of the leverage approach.

If there is anything new to privatization, it is this emphasis on leveraging private behavior with targeted public policy. The growth of the nonprofit sector and the availability of privatized government-like services makes it possible for government, in the words of Osborne and Gaebler (1992), to "steer rather than row." Government, in this sense, is not the only organization available to implement public policy, but it does have primary responsibility for creating the policy that is to be implemented. This approach not only shifts some of the burden for service delivery away from government, but as some would argue it allows for government to take on a more appropriate role of policy creator rather than service provider.

Benefits of Privatization

The issue of privatization is often accompanied by a great deal of ideological baggage about the relative value and competence of the government in comparison with the private sector. Many of privatization's most ardent supporters believe that smaller government is a benefit in and of itself. We believe that the decision to privatize should be analyzed without a preconceived notion that privatization is the better way until proved otherwise. This requires a case-by-case, rational analysis of the benefits and costs of privatization for each individual instance of the make-or-buy decision.

The greatest benefit of privatization is that it opens up the possibility of competition in the performance of a public function. This is not to say that competition is a cure-all. There are some instances when competition is not possible or desirable. As Kettl (1993) points out, although competition can enhance efficiency in the provision of public services and products, efficiency is only one goal of government. Competition, he says, "does not capture—and, indeed, can slight—a vast array of other goals that have equal or sometimes greater priority" (p. 6). In many cases, however, services and programs that are higher in quality and lower in cost are delivered when organizations compete for the business; customer choice can be maximized as well. According to Osborne and Gaebler (1992, p. 92), this is because "competition does not wait for good management: if managers cannot keep costs down and improve quality, their customers go elsewhere and they go out of business." Whether the customer is buying a car or selecting a garbage pickup service, the incentives for the provider that were put in place by competition hold. Another benefit of competition is that it can inspire innovation in service delivery (Osborne and Gaebler, 1992; Kent and Wooten, 1987).

Privatization can facilitate organizational differentiation and focus. One of the great problems of a direct government program is the public investment required to create the organizational capacity to field the program. Once the capacity is created, it develops its own dynamic and seeks to preserve itself. If the policy design behind the program is flawed, it is very difficult for a large-scale government program to dismantle the old experiment and begin a new one. For one thing, the legislation creating the program may not provide the flexibility. For another, the people who make up the organization may not have the skills to implement the new program. Just as business people prefer to run companies using other people's money, there is a benefit to government programs that are implemented using other people's organizational capacity.

Privatization therefore enables public managers to focus on policy design and program evaluation, and allows other organizations—possibly with more organizational capacity and expertise in a given area—to worry about the direct administration of governmental programs. In the case of the New York City housing tax incentive program, government officials created public policy to strongly encourage developers to improve and enhance the City's low-income housing stock instead of involving public employees in the actual construction and operation of housing units. This freedom allows government officials to concentrate on their distinctive competence—crafting sound public policy—rather than on the often highly technical aspects of day-to-day program administration.

Selling off government-owned businesses raises a very different set of issues and brings a different set of benefits than contracting out, leveraging, or entering into a public-private partnership. At the heart of this form of privatization is a narrowing of the definition of the public sector and an expansion of the sphere of what is defined as private. With socialism, nations decided that the material well-being of a society was a central focus of public policy. If the free market was not investing in air transport, telecommunications, nuclear power, or auto manufacturing, then government had to make sure that these industries were developed, *even if they had to do it themselves.*

The advantage of this strategy was that some of the nation's resources were directed toward the creation of modern industrial infrastructure and production. This had the positive effect of creating employment and wealth, and sometimes producing new technologies. The flaw in the strategy was that while some short-term benefits resulted from these social investments and modernization efforts, in the long run many of these enterprises became inefficient—and at times corrupt—bureaucratic monopolies. In the days before a world economy, these inefficient enterprises were protected from global competition by the state. As trade barriers become obsolete in an emerging world economy, these state-owned enterprises are unable to compete, and they require even larger government subsidies to survive.

The major benefit of privatization through the sale of state-owned enterprises is that new forms of management and technology and new sources of capital are generated and applied to production. This lowers the costs of production and increases the generation of wealth. Here again we see the ability of privatization to spur innovative approaches to service delivery, and in the end a higher standard of living. Further, this form of privatization may be politically popular and could become a quick victory for public managers who wish to privatize.

As Van Oudenhoven (1989, p. 179) points out, "For politicians, the privatization of state enterprises is a relatively pleasant measure. Essentially, it is just a matter of selling state assets and receiving money in the bargain." The sale of state-owned assets in the former East Germany infused its new market economy with more than $170 billion. This form of privatization can reduce the costs of government while simultaneously providing revenue, if only in one shot, for the governmental unit.

Costs of Privatization

The principal costs of privatization stem from the loss of direct government control over program administration. With any form of privatization, the production of goods and services needed to implement public policy is no longer in the hands of government. This results in a situation wherein government officials cannot easily issue to their subordinates directives designed to affect quality of service. As Kettl (1993, p. 22) notes, "They can threaten, cajole, or persuade, but in the end, they can only shape the incentives to which the contractors respond."

If one private entity develops monopoly control of a service, or dominates that industry and holds a quasi monopoly, government's ability to influence program implementation may be further compromised. And just as public sector monopolies lead to ineffi-cient and low-quality service, so too do contractor monopolies. After privatization, the skills and knowledge gained through pro-gram administration belong to the private firm and not to the government. Government may come to lack the technical exper-tise or knowledge base to effectively manage its private partners. This is an especially urgent problem if, in the future, the govern-ment is required by legislation, public opinion, the collapse of a private contractor, or other equally compelling forces to resume direct delivery of the product or service they chose to privatize. In a large free-market economy such as the United States, tens of thousands of private businesses fail every year.

Another possible disadvantage of privatization is the discon-nection it creates between the formulation of public policy and day-to-day program operational concerns. Conceptually, policy for-mulation and program implementation are interconnected. Pol-icy design must account for organizational capacity, available expertise, financial feasibility, and other operational details. Designing public policy that leads to effective program imple-mentation requires knowledge of administrative issues and the abil-ity to influence administrative behavior. A reduced understanding of administrative issues and reduced leverage over implementation behaviors is a cost of privatization. Therefore, privatization requires that extra effort, time, and resources be devoted to ensuring effec-tive communication between the policy design world and those who will be responsible for implementing the policy.

A related financial cost of privatization is the cost of establish-ing management controls and bidding procedures; in fact, con-tract monitoring has been called the "most arduous and expensive part of the process" (Praeger, 1994, p. 181). Regardless which entity is actually executing the delivery of a public service, the responsibility and accountability for public policy and its imple-mentation remain with the government.

Tasks associated with contract management include develop-ing requests for proposals and communicating the requests to potential bidders. In addition, organization must develop man-agement controls to ensure that the contractor's work conforms to public policy and results in desired outputs and outcomes. These controls will include reporting procedures, inspections, audits, and meetings to ensure that the work meets government's expectations.

Osborne and Gaebler (1992, p. 87) suggest that "to do it right, cities often spend 20 percent of the cost of the service on contract management" and "typically have to hire new people, with particular expertise" for contract management. These resource issues— financial and otherwise—must be considered in conjunction with the financial savings and other potential benefits brought about by privatization. At any rate, neither an elected nor an unelected leader will get very far with the excuse that "the contractor messed up and it's not our fault."

A good example of this danger is found in the administration of foster care services in New York City. In a city as large and diverse as New York, foster care is a major responsibility for local government. For some time, under several mayors, a good portion of the actual monitoring of the quality of care provided by foster parents has been contracted out to private, nonprofit organizations. Not surprisingly, when a tragedy occurs, the media is quick to demand that the government explain what went wrong and why, and to assess blame. When Mayor Rudolph Giuliani ran against then Mayor David Dinkins in 1993, he was highly critical of the city's management of the foster care system. Candidate Giuliani stressed that the mayor was ultimately responsible for the well-being of the foster care children, regardless of what organization was actually delivering the service or monitoring the quality of care. And he indicated that given the past performance of city agencies in this area, more contracting out to private organizations should be done and would be done if he were elected.

In 1997, when a child was beaten to death by foster parents, Mayor Giuliani informed the media that a nonprofit organization under contract with the city was responsible for monitoring the case and that the blame was theirs. The mayor suggested that the press seek answers from the private organization, not from him or his administration. Not surprisingly, the media strongly disagreed with the mayor's assessment, choosing to hold his administration accountable for the tragedy, regardless of whether the monitoring was the direct responsibility of a city agency or of a private firm under contract with the city.

The sale of state-owned enterprises also brings with it a variety of costs. First and foremost is human dislocation resulting from unemployment. For this reason, privatization schemes often face major opposition from public employee groups (Savas, 1987).

While this is also a cost of U.S.-style contracting out of government functions, very often private firms have been required or encouraged to attempt to employ the government workers who previously performed these tasks. In the case of divestment privatization, the elimination of employment tends to be more widespread and the social impacts are far more profound. Again, the example of the Treuhandanstalt is a striking one. The social unrest resulting in part from the privatization of the East German economy was great, and ultimately led to the assassination of Detlev Rohwedder, the one-time head of the Treuhandanstalt.

Defenders of privatization argue that these dislocations are short-term pain that will lead to long-term gain. While this may sometimes be true, it brings to mind the traditional distinction between a depression and a recession: a recession is when you lose your job, a depression is when I lose mine. It is arguable that the role of government is not to guarantee jobs or financial security to public employees, but it is also true that the costs—political, social, and financial—of human displacement associated with privatization schemes are very real.

A very unfortunate cost of privatization is that government's role in economic development has been delegitimized. Although some would like to believe that the market can do everything, the fact is that it cannot, and the hidden hand may not achieve desired social objectives. The flaw in the socialist strategy of state ownership may not have been that the state helped create industry, but rather that the state insisted on managing industry and managing it as a monopoly. Government can help create the conditions that permit technologies and industries to develop. The Internet started in the U.S. Defense Department. The minicomputer was developed for the space program. Government can provide capital, infrastructure, research and development funding, and tax advantages that stimulate economic development. Though we have learned that this is best done in a competitive environment, we have also learned the advantages of, and the inevitability of, mixed economies.

Overall, a major cost of privatization is that the advantages of mixed economies are being lost in a fog of ideological near-worship of the glory of the market. As Van Oudenhoven (1989, p. 163) notes, "For most governments, privatization has become a goal in itself instead of a means." This ideological and undiscriminating application of privatization is simply unwise.

Part Two

Learning from Public Sector Cases

Chapter Eight

Management Innovation in the New York City Department of Parks and Recreation

What follows is a case study of an effort spanning nearly a decade to implement a variety of management innovation techniques in New York City's Department of Parks and Recreation (DPR). These innovations were implemented by two recent parks commissioners, primarily in response to increased fiscal austerity. The case begins during the mayoral administration of David Dinkins and his parks commissioner, Betsy Gotbaum, and continues through the first term of Mayor Rudolph Giuliani and his parks commissioner, Henry Stern. Commissioner Gotbaum's primary innovations involved Total Quality Management (TQM) and targeted efforts at public-private partnerships to generate private resources for the parks. Commissioner Stern, who is still in office at this writing, has experimented with privatization, performance management systems, and the use of welfare workers to perform specific tasks within parks operations.

This case both allows the reader to become familiar with the mechanics of implementing such innovations as TQM, performance management systems, and public-private partnerships, and elucidates some central issues that influence the success of any management innovation attempt.

Introduction

The mission of New York City's DPR is to ensure that the city's parks, beaches, playgrounds, stadia, marinas, recreation facilities, gardens, malls, squares, and public spaces are clean, safe, and attractive for the health and enjoyment of the citizenry. In pursuit of this mission, the DPR has established the following goals:

- Improve the condition of parks and playgrounds
- Increase the number and improve the condition of the city's street trees and natural areas
- Provide venues for recreational activities
- Develop public-private partnerships aimed at garnering resources for the department

According to a survey administered by the Commonwealth Fund in 1994, the residents of New York City strongly support the DPR's mission. Survey results reflect that a solid majority of New Yorkers (62 percent) believe that parks are as essential as police protection, fire protection, and sanitation. In addition, 96 percent of survey respondents indicated that parks make New York a more livable city, and that safe, open spaces in which children can play are essential to child development (Commonwealth Fund, 1994).

Although a broad consensus exists that clean, safe parks and recreational opportunities are essential to the quality of life in New York, there is less agreement about the manner in which the DPR should operationalize its mission, and about the level of resources the city should devote to the implementation of its parks and recreation program.

History

The first major expansion of public park space occurred in the late nineteenth century when Frederick Law Olmstead and Calvert Vaux designed Central Park in Manhattan (in 1858), and Prospect Park in the then-separate city of Brooklyn (in 1865). Shortly thereafter (in 1872), Olmstead designed Riverside Park, and the city acquired 3,495 acres of parkland, including St. Mary's, Claremont, Crotona, Bronx, Van Cortlandt, and Pelham Bay Parks.

In the early twentieth century, acquisition of new parkland slowed. Instead of focusing on land acquisition and park construction, the DPR concentrated on enhancing existing park facilities with playgrounds and recreational opportunities for children. During the rule of the Tammany Hall political machine in the 1920s, the condition and upkeep of public parks and recreational facilities decreased dramatically.

Robert Moses, who served as parks commissioner from 1934 to 1960, reversed this trend dramatically. During Moses's reign, park space more than doubled, beaches were renovated and rebuilt, and the department built hundreds of new recreational facilities. This expansionary trend continued for a decade after Moses's tenure, and ended with New York City's fiscal crisis during the 1970s. From the 1970s to the 1990s, the DPR concentrated on maintaining the parks and recreational facilities that already existed.

Recently, under the leadership of Commissioner Stern, the DPR has quietly resumed acquisition of park space. According to DPR Chief of Staff Ian Shapiro, the city acquired 527 acres of parkland during 1994.

Current Physical Assets

Presently, the New York City parks system consists of more than 27,000 acres of parkland and other properties. Parks account for almost 20,000 acres, while nonpark properties make up the remainder (Brecher and Mead, 1991). Nonpark properties include playgrounds; expressway and parkway land; malls, strips, and plots; circles, squares, and triangles; and miscellaneous other properties.

New York City's park system is large and multifaceted. The DPR runs 479 parks. Its five best-known parks (Central Park in Manhattan, Flushing Meadows-Corona in Queens, Prospect Park in Brooklyn, Van Cortlandt-Pelham Bay in the Bronx, and the Greenbelt in Staten Island) constitute more than 40 percent of total park acreage. In addition to these five flagship parks, thirty-four parks take up 100 acres each, accounting for a total of 8,385 acres, approximately 43 percent of all parkland. Thus thirty-nine large parks account for approximately 84 percent of parkland, and forty-one medium-sized parks (20 to 100 acres) and 399 small parks (under 20 acres) account for the remaining 16 percent (3,072 acres). Park facilities also include 623 ball fields, 541 tennis courts, 33 outdoor swimming pools, 10 indoor swimming pools, 31 recreation and senior centers, 14 miles of beaches, 13 golf courses, 6 ice rinks, 4 major stadiums, and 5 zoos (Brecher and Mead, 1991). When this park system was built, the government had a large number of low-wage workers. Today the DPR faces the challenge of managing its huge system with declining resources.

Current Operational Trends

The DPR devotes the preponderance of its resources to operations—that is, to the management and maintenance of parks and facilities. Daily maintenance activities include removing graffiti, picking up litter and trash, mowing grass, planting and pruning trees, removing dead trees and stumps, and repairing park benches, playground equipment, and other facilities. The DPR also devotes a significant amount of resources to operations-related technical services such as vehicle maintenance and specialized equipment repairs. Commissioner Gotbaum would often remark that two of the main tasks of the department were to pick up garbage and to cut the grass. In addition to providing daily operations and maintenance services, the DPR staffs pools and recreation centers, and sponsors more than five hundred major recreational events annually (although the agency's recreational programming is focused largely outside the sponsorship of such events, despite this seemingly large number of them; the primary focus of the DPR's recreational program is daily programming in hundreds of facilities).

In 1995, the DPR initiated more than 150 construction projects in the city's park space. Nearly all of these projects involved reconstruction of park and playground facilities, although the department also broke ground on a small number of new playgrounds as part of this surge in construction.

Comparison with Parks Programs in Other Major U.S. Cities

Compared with parks programs in other major U.S. cities, New York City's program is extensive (see Exhibit 8.1). A 1991 study by the Citizens Budget Commission contained a survey of fourteen

Exhibit 8.1. Local Public Parkland in Selected U.S. Cities.

Selected Cities	Park Acreage as % of Total Land	Park Acreage per 10,000 residents
Baltimore	12.3%	85
Chicago	5	24
Dallas	9.2	201
Detroit	6.8	54
Houston	5.3	111
Indianapolis	4.1	131
Los Angeles	5	48
New York City	13.5	36
Philadelphia	11.4	60
Phoenix	11.9	345
San Antonio	3.4	71
San Diego	3.9	84
San Francisco	11.1	46
San Jose	3.7	58
Mean	7.6	96.7
Median	6.05	65.5
NYC Rank	1 of 14	13 of 14

Source: Brecher and Mead, *Managing the Department of Parks and Recreation in a Period of Fiscal Stress,* Citizens Budget Commission, 1991, p. 10.

major U.S. cities, including New York City (Brecher and Mead, 1991, p. 10). Of the cities surveyed, only Phoenix possessed more parkland acreage than New York in absolute terms, and New York City devoted the highest percentage of its total land (13.5 percent) to parks.

The city of New York, however, has a higher population density than any other major city in the United States; the implication of this is that New Yorkers have less parkland to share than residents of other major metropolitan areas across the country. Among the cities included in the survey, only Chicago possessed less acreage per 10,000 citizens than New York City. New Yorkers have 36 park acres per ten thousand residents, while the average among the fourteen cities surveyed was 96.7 acres per ten thousand citizens.

The Budget

The adopted budget of the City of New York for fiscal year 1995 allocated approximately $150 million for operating expenditures and provided $165 million for spending on capital projects (see Exhibit 8.2). This budget reflected a decrease of 5.2 percent in the total parks budget compared with the previous fiscal year. The DPR estimates that actual operating expenditures in 1995 were closer to $161 million, while actual capital expenditures were about $99 million. Of the expenses provided for in the 1995 adopted budget, 78 percent were devoted to maintenance and operations.

Clearly, the DPR devotes the majority of its resources to the maintenance and operation of existing facilities, despite the fact that the budget for maintenance and operations decreased by 4.8 percent from 1994 to 1995. The high priority awarded to maintenance and operations in the DPR's budget corresponds directly to the public's desire for clean, safe parks. In a survey of park users conducted by the authors (Cohen and Eimicke, 1996), nearly 85 percent of the respondents viewed cleanliness and safety as "essential" attributes of park quality. Another 67 percent viewed maintenance of play equipment and facilities as essential.

Since 1990, the DPR's budget has decreased by 23 percent in real terms. In fact, public operating expenditures for parks and

Exhibit 8.2. Department of Parks and Recreation Adopted Budget Summary.

Budget Types	FY 1995 (in Thousands of Dollars)
Expense Budget (Gross)[a]	150,156
Capital Budget	165,633
Revenue Budget (Gross)[a]	41,249

[a]Budgets are gross of intracity revenues and expenses.

Source: Adopted Budget, Fiscal Year 1995, New York City.

recreation are at their lowest level since before 1965 (see Exhibit 8.3). Capital expenditures, at $99 million, fell by 42 percent from 1990 to 1995 (see Exhibit 8.4). Capital expenditures for 1996 and 1997, however, show significant increases at $155 million and $175 million respectively.

In addition to decreasing in absolute terms, the resource levels devoted to New York City parks lag behind spending on parks programs in other major U.S. cities. Exhibit 8.5 compares the 1991 park expenditures of eighteen cities across three measures: operating expenditures as a percentage of the city operating budget, park expenditures per capita, and park expenditures per acre of parkland. New York ranks below the eighteen-city average for each of these three benchmarks, and falls below the median for park

Exhibit 8.3. Department of Parks and Recreation Operating Expenditures: Selected Fiscal Years 1945–1995.

Fiscal Year	Operating Expenditures in Current Dollars (in Thousands of Dollars)	Operating Expenditures in Constant (1983) Dollars (in Thousands of Dollars)	% Change over 5 years
1945	10,739.8	55,736.7	—
1950	16,390.8	65,105.1	17%
1955	24,365.6	86,741.4	33
1960	28,763.9	92,991.9	7
1965	38,321.2	115,353.8	24
1970	52,605.7	128,990.5	12
1975	75,948.7	132,599.5	3
1980	104,200.5	130,191.3	−2
1985	148,260.4	135,057.0	4
1990	178,719.0	129,409.4	−4
1995	161,500.0	99,568.4	−23

Note: Converted to constant (1983) dollars using CPI-Urban, New York, New York-Northeastern N.J. from the Bureau of Labor Statistics.

Sources: Brecher and Mead, *Managing the Department of Parks and Recreation in a Period of Fiscal Stress,* Citizens Budget Commission, 1991, p. 15; Adopted Budget, Fiscal Year 1995, New York City.

**Exhibit 8.4. Department of Parks and Recreation
Capital Expenditures: Selected Fiscal Years 1945–1995.**

Fiscal Year	Capital Expenditures in Current Dollars (in Millions of Dollars)	Capital Expenditures in Constant (1983) Dollars (in Millions of Dollars)	% Change over 5 years
1945	1.8	9.3	—
1950	4.8	19.1	104.1%
1955	7.7	27.4	43.8
1960	8.1	26.2	−4.5
1965	26.2	78.9	201.2
1970	34.1	83.6	6.0
1975	51.4	89.7	7.3
1980	29.6	37.0	−58.8
1985	91.2	83.1	124.6
1990	145.4	105.3	26.7
1995	99.0	61.0	−42.0

Note: Converted to constant (1983) dollars using CPI-Urban, New York, New York-Northeastern N.J. from the Bureau of Labor Statistics.

Sources: Brecher and Mead, *Managing the Department of Parks and Recreation in a Period of Fiscal Stress,* Citizens Budget Commission, 1991, p. 15; Adopted Budget, Fiscal Year 1995, New York City.

expenditures as a percentage of the city budget, and for park expenditures per capita. In fact, New York ranks 18th out of 18, and 17th out of 18 for these measures, respectively.

Utilization

Although the use levels of New York City parks by city residents are not studied regularly, a number of studies have attempted to estimate park use. A 1991 study by the Citizens Budget Commission reported a number of utilization estimates based on several previous studies (Brecher and Mead, 1991). In addition, a rigorous study of Riverside Park by Ukeles and Associates (1991) estimated use levels for that particular park. These studies provide an indication of

Exhibit 8.5. Parks Expenditures in Selected U.S. Cities, 1991.

Selected Cities	Parks Operating Budget as % of City's Total Operating Budget	Parks Operating Expenditures per Capita	Parks Operating Expenditures per Acre
Baltimore	1.9	47.0	5.3
Boston	2.0	24.4	5.2
Buffalo	0.9	15.9	3.7
Chicago	6.2	72.3	27.2
Cincinnati	3.4	56.0	4.1
Cleveland	3.9	55.4	14.7
Dallas	3.4	38.6	2.0
Detroit	2.8	57.5	9.9
Houston	5.6	30.7	1.6
Kansas City	5.7	73.5	3.2
Los Angeles	3.4	38.2	8.9
Milwaukee	5.0	37.1	2.4
New York City	0.4	17.4	4.9
Philadelphia	1.3	18.7	3.4
Phoenix	8.1	40.8	1.3
Pittsburgh	5.4	48.8	7.2
San Antonio	3.0	29.9	4.3
St. Louis	3.8	29.2	3.9
Mean	3.7	40.6	6.3
Median	3.4	38.4	4.2
NYC Rank	18 of 18	17 of 18	8 of 18

Source: Parks Council and Central Park Conservancy, 1993.

the extensive use that New Yorkers and visitors to the city make of the parks. Exhibit 8.6 reports these utilization estimates.

Innovation Through TQM in Response to Budget Cuts

New York City clearly has an expansive and heavily utilized parks system. In a society in which leisure time has become scarcer, and therefore more highly valued, citizens increasingly consider recreational resources a vital part of the urban infrastructure. As already indicated, New York City's park system has suffered from significant resource constraints since the mid-1960s. The Giuliani administration only recently has begun to reverse this trend. The remainder of this chapter presents the innovation efforts, undertaken in response to the resource scarcity experienced by the DPR, of the past two parks commissioners, who have served since 1990.

Betsy Gotbaum took office as parks commissioner on February 5, 1990, only one month after the inauguration of Mayor David Dinkins. At that time, Mayor Dinkins's top priorities included public safety and education. His agenda proved detrimental to the level of resources available to Commissioner Gotbaum and the DPR, and the mayor's priorities ultimately required Gotbaum to embrace substantial cuts in the agency's budget. The cuts resulted in a hiring freeze, layoffs, and furloughs of park employees. Union representatives reacted furiously, staging a demonstration at city

Exhibit 8.6. Park Utilization Estimates.

Park Name	Use Estimate (Visits)	Source	Year
Central Park	14,200,000 (by 3,000,000 users)	Kornblum and Williams	1982
Van Cortlandt	763,000	Meyersohn	1986
Pelham Bay	1,000,000	Meyersohn	1987
Prospect Park	4,370,000	Meyersohn	1987
Riverside Park	2,865,000	Ukeles and Associates	1991

Sources: Brecher and Mead, *Managing the Department of Parks and Recreation in a Period of Fiscal Stress,* Citizens Budget Commission, 1991, pp. 28–31; Ukeles Associates, Inc., *The Users of Riverside Park.* New York: Riverside Park Fund, 1991, p. 3.

hall and condemning the cuts in general and the commissioner specifically.

In an effort to cope with the cuts and still maintain one of the largest and most complex urban park systems in the world, Gotbaum pursued four key strategies. Her approach involved

1. Conducting tough, behind-the-scenes battles with the Office of Management and Budget to restore some of the cuts
2. Negotiating agreements with the union to share in the benefits of new revenue-generating initiatives
3. Gaining flexibility in the application of the cuts in order to minimize reductions of maintenance personnel
4. Soliciting funds and in-kind support from parks-oriented nonprofit organizations and foundations

In addition to these tactics, Gotbaum adopted TQM in an effort to "do more with less." The commissioner's conversion to TQM as a management philosophy began with training sessions for her senior executives. The sessions were conducted by members of private corporations who successfully employed TQM at their businesses.

Although it pleased Gotbaum that a substantial number of her senior managers were knowledgeable about the techniques and philosophy of TQM, she believed that prepackaged TQM training lacked the efficacy to make TQM a functioning reality in the DPR. She acquired a grant to develop a hands-on TQM training and implementation program designed specifically for the DPR, and then asked her two TQM managers, Assistant Commissioner Edward Norris and Quality Coordinator Warren DeLuca, to engage consultants to facilitate the effort. After some research, Norris and DeLuca interviewed a Columbia faculty team and subsequently invited the team to submit a detailed proposal in early May 1992. In spring 1992, Commissioner Gotbaum engaged Columbia University professors and TQM consultants Steven Cohen, William Eimicke, and Jacob Ukeles to help her implement TQM at the DPR.

The proposal submitted by the Columbia faculty team contained the following key points.

- *TQM consists of three core concepts:*

1. Supplies utilized in work processes must be designed specifically for use.
2. Staff analysis of work processes must be undertaken to improve routine organizational functions and reduce process variation.
3. Close communication with customers helps to identify and understand what they want and how they define quality.

- *Engendering genuine organizational change under any circumstances is difficult and, given a series of management fads, workers are bound to be skeptical.* The Columbia consulting team pointed out that one of the drawbacks of TQM is the religious fervor of many followers of W. Edwards Deming, the original TQM guru. They warned that this factor could turn off DPR employees in advance. The consulting team assured DPR leadership that although some employee skepticism might be warranted, TQM had significant intrinsic value. They predicted that if the department made an overriding commitment to quality management, the merits of TQM would lead to its success.
- *The project-oriented approach is more effective than traditionally implemented TQM because it introduces TQM gradually.* The Columbia faculty team's approach to TQM implementation was to train senior managers in the core concepts of TQM; to identify a small group of those exposed to TQM who are enthusiastic or, at a minimum, open to change; and to work with that group to provide them with the tools and mechanisms for bringing TQM to their staff. This approach is in contrast to traditional TQM implementation, which is typically done on an organizationwide basis. The Columbia team has found that their approach is a more effective means to implement TQM, particularly in public sector and nonprofit organizations.

To begin the project, the Columbia team suggested a process for selecting the senior managers who would receive TQM training and outlined the content of the training. Each borough office and major headquarters unit—a total of eight units—selected a quality coordinator. In most cases this coordinator was the unit head's chief deputy. These coordinators and their senior managers received training in the basics of TQM. This training provided a definition of TQM, methods for selecting quality improvement projects and project teams, and strategies for managing quality teams and building a TQM organization

After the initial training and with the assistance of Norris, DeLuca, and the consultant team, the senior managers moved forward in implementing TQM in their units. This approach reflected the consulting team's philosophy that further training would amount to waste unless incorporated into the overall strategy to make TQM a part of the organization's daily operational routine.

Implementing TQM at Parks: Learning by Doing

The Columbia faculty termed their approach to TQM "learning by doing." In this approach, seminars and videos about TQM have less impact on an organization's way of completing its work than assignments that require an understanding of TQM. In New York City's DPR, the consulting team initially taught TQM by helping the department to undertake two dozen quality improvement projects. One purpose of these first projects was to garner some quick victories for TQM. The main purpose of the initial quality improvement projects, however, was to teach TQM by revising the DPR's approach to work, to ingrain the ideals of TQM in DPR staff by asking them to work according to TQM precepts.

In other words, rather than providing extensive abstract training on TQM, the commissioner issued assignments to the rank and file that could not be completed unless they understood TQM. This approach motivated staff members to learn that TQM was not just a bunch of academic ideas but a body of knowledge critical to completing an important assignment from the boss.

The strategy executed by the DPR was very similar to the one initially proposed by the Columbia faculty team, and included the following elements.

1. For each of the eight borough and headquarters units, the commissioner appointed a quality coordinator. In every case these coordinators were respected and influential senior staff members.

2. Coordinators attended three instructional briefings on the core concepts of TQM: how to do work analysis, how to identify improvement projects, and how to initiate and manage improvement teams.

3. Quality coordinators and their supervisors participated in a full-day meeting to discuss the management of improvement projects.

4. Commissioner Gotbaum required each unit to identify three quality improvement projects and submit them for approval within ten days of the conclusion of the initial training cycle.

5. TQM consultants were assigned to each borough and head-quarters unit to provide whatever help the units required to complete their initial improvement projects.

Although each borough and headquarters unit that undertook a quality project had access to a consultant who provided whatever implementation assistance became necessary, quality teams generally did not utilize the assistance offered by consulting staff after an initial meeting or two. In most cases, the line workers and their managers appeared reluctant to utilize consultant help because of their concern that such use would increase oversight by the headquarters.

During the first stage of TQM implementation at the DPR, Columbia faculty trained 25 people. In the second stage, more than 120 employees learned TQM by working on another round of improvement projects. The third phase included an additional 50 managers receiving training, and 250 employees learned TQM by working on the department's third round of fifty improvement projects. TQM training took place on an as-needed basis to complete the commissioner's quality improvement assignments.

A key step in the implementation of TQM at the DPR was a decision by then Deputy Commissioner William Dalton to include reviews of the department's quality improvement projects at his weekly senior management operations meetings. He asked DeLuca, the department's quality coordinator, to provide him with a weekly report on the status of each project. These reports became the basis for discussion of projects at the regular operations meeting—Dalton would question managers concerning the progress or delays of various initiatives. Parks managers also used this time to supplement TQM training and to share positive and negative experiences in team activity. In this manner, Deputy Commissioner Dalton kept projects moving. For projects that did not exhibit progress, Dalton established a time frame for improvement and progress. If a certain project did not reach successful completion by the end of this time frame, the project was dissolved and reevaluated.

Assessing Costs and Benefits of the First TQM Projects

As emphasized throughout this section of the case, the central proposition of the DPR's TQM strategy was the belief that ensuring quality must ultimately become the way an organization operates. Initial projects assigned by the commissioner enabled staff to learn this new strategy by implementing it. Though these efforts provided the department with some quick victories, more important they allowed the staff to integrate the TQM concept of quality into their daily work on the implementation of these projects.

An analysis of ten of the first twenty-four projects conducted by a group of Columbia University graduate students of public policy and administration illustrated the financial and operational benefits of TQM at the DPR. Start-up costs totaled $223,000, or approximately $23,000 per project. Savings totaled $711,500, or approximately $71,000 on an annual, per project basis. Based on average project savings at the time of the study, recurring annual savings were projected to total $1.7 million. This figure did not include indirect and long-term benefits but simply the direct annual savings of each project. Exhibit 8.7 summarizes the findings of this study and provides data on the savings of ten of the initial twenty-four projects. Though these productivity gains were significant benefits of the process of organizational change, the main purpose of the first projects was to teach TQM to DPR staff.

Maintaining Momentum: A Challenge

At the end of the DPR's first year of TQM, the department could boast of a number of successes, but department leaders were uncertain about how to proceed. DeLuca, the department's quality coordinator, expressed his concern that senior managers appeared

Exhibit 8.7. Dollar Savings from DPR Sample Quality Projects.

Project	Estimated Annual Savings
Preventative Maintenance Inspection: Randall's Island	$106,000
Citywide Time Keeping	97,000
Central Park Rodent Problem	0
Brooklyn Mobile Parks Cleanup Crews	20,700
Bronx Specialized Equipment Team	228,800
Queens Forestry Department Tree Removal	114,000
Maintenance of Bronx Ball Fields	(25,000)
Manhattan Garbage Disposal	170,000
Central Park Tennis Court Administration	0
Reduction in Change Order Approval Time	0
Total Savings	$711,500

Source: Dunn and others, 1993, p. 1.

less supportive of TQM than they had been initially. In response to this concern, DeLuca met with the Columbia faculty team and asked them to propose a series of next steps that would facilitate the acceptance of TQM at the DPR. A memo from the consulting team proposed a quarterly review process and a number of other steps designed to renew the TQM initiative's momentum.

Taking TQM Out of the DPR

After receiving the proposal from the Columbia faculty consultants, Deputy Commissioner Dalton employed the recommendations and proceeded with the first quarterly review meetings in October 1993. At the meetings, each organizational unit outlined plans for the next quarter. These plans included specific commitments to quality improvements that the unit intended to undertake. The deputy commissioners and borough commissioners also submitted progress memos to Dalton, and private meetings took place with each deputy commissioner and Dalton, DeLuca, Norris, Cohen, and Eimicke to review the status of TQM implementation in each organizational unit.

In fall 1993, a mayoral campaign was under way. The mayoral election served as a backdrop during the first round of review meetings, and ultimately the results of that election halted DPR's TQM initiative. Candidate Rudolph Giuliani defeated incumbent Mayor Dinkins in the mayoral race, and because the position of parks commissioner is a political appointment, the Giuliani victory had significant implications for Betsy Gotbaum, her staff, and the future of her department. During fall 1993, as the staff discussed their department's uncertain future, the TQM initiative remained a priority with department leaders, and the first quarterly review meetings were successfully completed.

The election of Giuliani resulted in an overhauling of the administration and personnel of most city agencies, including the DPR. After the new mayor was inaugurated, the TQM implementation project was halted. Shortly thereafter, Commissioner Gotbaum and a number of her key aides resigned. Commissioner Gotbaum was replaced by Henry Stern, who had served as parks commissioner in the Koch administration, immediately prior to Dinkins's election.

Mayor Giuliani, who ran on a reinvention platform, supported the implementation of innovative management techniques in city agencies. Newly appointed Commissioner Stern embraced this philosophy; however, though he did not criticize the efforts of the TQM project established by his predecessor, he did not continue it, and he viewed TQM as a priority of his predecessor that he could ignore.

A large number of DPR staff had never fully understood or agreed with the philosophy of TQM and considered it as nothing more than one of the vestiges of the Gotbaum era. For these staff members, the return of Henry Stern was a relief—now it would be possible to return to the "old way" of working.

Unfortunately, the round of cutbacks at the DPR had not ended, and Commissioner Stern faced an even bleaker budget situation than that faced by Commissioner Gotbaum nearly five years earlier. Stern's response to the cutbacks included a renewed effort to raise private charitable donations for the parks, an effort to raise additional revenue from private advertisements on parkland, increased use of welfare workers to perform basic maintenance duties, targeted privatization of cleanup and maintenance services, and increased use of performance management reporting systems. Commissioner Stern did not consider reviving TQM as a means to mitigate the budget reductions.

Innovation Through Enhancement and Increased Utilization of Performance Measurement

A key strategy utilized by the DPR under Commissioner Stern was the use of park inspections to increase the day-to-day accountability of on-site parks managers. Just as the police department consulted geographic crime data to focus management attention on crime reduction strategies, so too would Commissioner Stern consult parks inspection data to target problems and direct the activities of his staff. He ordered an increase in the number and frequency of park inspections.

The expansion of the park inspection program was made feasible through the use of handheld computers to record inspection data. These computers, which inspectors utilize during the on-site inspections, facilitate the swift compilation of inspection results. In 1992, 1993, and 1994 combined, fourteen hundred park inspections were conducted. In 1995, that three-year total was exceeded by six hundred inspections, as DPR staff logged two thousand inspections that year (New York City Department of Parks and Recreation, 1996b).

The increased use of performance data is still an operational strategy at DPR. The system used by department managers to evaluate the quality and upkeep of parks and park facilities is called the Parks Inspection Program (PIP). DPR's Office of Operations and Management Planning uses PIP to rate the cleanliness and condition of every park site of six or fewer acres. (Parks of more than six acres are also included in the inspection program, but at these larger parks only specific sites, mostly playgrounds, are eligible for inspection.) They also inspect all playgrounds, sitting areas, and public triangles and squares. Inspections are conducted on a biweekly basis.

The PIP rates parks as acceptable or unacceptable in two categories: *cleanliness* and *overall condition*. The cleanliness rating consists of the following features: graffiti, glass, lawns, litter, and weeds. The overall condition rating consists of the five cleanliness features plus seven structural features: sidewalks, safety surfaces, paved surfaces, play equipment, trees, benches, and fences. Cleanliness is deemed acceptable if all of the following conditions are met:

1. Three of the five features are rated as acceptable.
2. The park does not have excessive glass in play areas.
3. No unsanitary conditions exist.
4. Overgrown weeds or grass do not prevent use of the site.

The overall condition of the park is deemed acceptable if

1. Ten of the twelve cleanliness and structural features are acceptable.
2. No deficiency exists that requires immediate attention, such as a safety hazard.

The standard for a park's overall condition is stricter than that for cleanliness, and if the cleanliness of the park is unacceptable, the overall condition of the park is unacceptable. (More specific rating criteria for each feature are published in DPR's *Parks Inspection Program Rating Guide for Small Parks, Playgrounds, Malls and Sitting Areas*. In general, these criteria are quite strict. For example, if a park is missing a garbage can or if a garbage can is overflowing, the park will receive a rating of unacceptable for the litter-garbage feature. Furthermore, any one immediate attention deficiency will cause a park to receive a rating of unacceptable for overall condition. Examples of immediate attention deficiencies include exposed park bench bolts, holes in the pavement, protruding sign stubs, downed or damaged fencing, splintered park bench slats, and fallen branches in play areas.)

Inspectors target sites at random, and park managers do not receive advance warning about inspections. Managers at the Office of Operations and Management Planning present the results of the inspections to the borough commissioners, as well as to the parks commissioner, at regular senior staff meetings. The results are also posted on a bulletin board located outside the parks commissioner's office.

Site managers of inspected parks also receive inspection data on a regular basis. In addition to the general inspection rating, park managers get detailed lists of deficiencies and Polaroid photographs of their site taken at the time of the inspection. The inspection report also breaks down the seriousness of each deficiency and advises what corrective action is required.

In addition, the PIP has a built-in method for correcting maintenance and cleanliness problems. Any unacceptable measures from the original inspection are reinspected after eight weeks. The results of these second inspections are presented to the first deputy commissioner and Commissioner Stern. The first deputy commissioner's staff independently tracks deficiencies involving potential safety hazards.

Impact of the Parks Inspection Program

The PIP has evolved into a highly effective performance management tool for DPR. The inspections notify park managers about what operational areas require improvement, and they establish maintenance priorities for the parks. The program also provides site managers with performance incentives. Ultimately, inspection results rate the effectiveness of park managers and borough offices. Park managers compete with one another for ratings and ratings improvements, and the five boroughs compete to have the best-maintained parks. Perhaps most important, the inspection program is an effective means of communicating DPR quality standards to park personnel and evaluating how well the personnel uphold these quality standards.

Improvement in cleanliness and overall condition ratings from 1994 to 1996 demonstrate the success of the PIP, despite budget and personnel reductions. Citywide, overall condition ratings increased from 39 percent acceptable in spring 1994 to 43 percent acceptable in spring 1995, and increased again to 62 percent acceptable in spring 1996 (see Exhibit 8.8). Citywide cleanliness ratings also increased dramatically. Although additional labor from welfare workers in the Work Experience Program and civic participation likely have had a role in these improvements, the PIP represents a systematic method for improving park cleanliness and maintenance over the long term and can be credited for much of the progress made in these areas over the last three years.

Exhibit 8.8. Parks Inspection Program Ratings by Borough.

Percentage Acceptable

	Overall Condition Rating		
Borough	*Spring 1994*	*Spring 1995*	*Spring 1996*
Bronx	27%	43%	53%
Brooklyn	35	38	57
Manhattan	41	41	67
Queens	46	45	61
Staten Island	50	58	91
Citywide	39	43	62

	Cleanliness Rating		
Borough	*Spring 1994*	*Spring 1995*	*Spring 1996*
Bronx	63%	77%	91%
Brooklyn	78	93	91
Manhattan	81	89	94
Queens	74	81	94
Staten Island	85	100	100
Citywide	75	86	93

Source: New York City Department of Parks and Recreation, 1996b.

Other Performance Measures

The Office of Operations and Management Planning also tracks quality measures that are not included in the PIP. These other measures include tree and stump removal and pruning, inspections of flagpoles and park signs, and the implementation of work productivity surveys. Operations and Management Planning staff have initiated an internal inspection program of recreation centers, which are evaluated twice a year, and beaches and pools, which are evaluated once each summer. The department also initiated a pilot program in which they conducted customer satisfaction surveys at recreation centers.

Despite the successes of the performance management program at DPR, a profound challenge facing the department's staff is the need to develop a method for inspecting the parts of parks of more than six acres that currently are excluded from the inspection program. Because medium-sized and large parks make up 84 percent of all parkland, most of the 27,000 acres of the city's parkland are not inspected. Recently the DPR drafted a plan to include all parks in the inspection program; unfortunately, at the time of this writing the DPR lacks the resources required to implement the plan.

Customer Perceptions of New York City Parks

The views of park users are a critical measure of departmental performance. Though customer surveys are not a regular element of the department's performance measurement system, the department is interested in information on customer satisfaction.

In summer 1996, the department cooperated with an experiment we proposed to pilot-test surveys of park users as a means of enhancing the performance measurement system. A team from Columbia University and a parks advocacy group known as the Parks Council conducted random surveys of 374 park users in ten New York City parks. This effort to obtain information on customer views received strong support from Commissioner Henry Stern, Parks Chief of Staff Ian Shapiro and, John Ifcher, the director of the department's Office of Operations and Management Planning. They agreed to cooperate in data collection efforts, and planned to utilize the information in operations planning.

Although operating expenditures by the DPR are generally lower than such expenditures in other major cities, and although operating expenditures have decreased in real terms since 1965, the public is fairly satisfied with the quality of New York City's parks. According to the survey we conducted in summer 1996, nearly 63 percent of park users rated the quality of the park they were visiting as either good or excellent. The 1994 Commonwealth Fund survey of a random sample of New York City residents had similarly found that 52 percent of New Yorkers gave a positive rating to park maintenance. Another 44 percent of respondents to the Commonwealth Fund survey believed that parks and playgrounds had improved over the previous five years.

In the aggregate, our survey reflects that most park users are reasonably satisfied with the parks. The most common response (43.6 percent) to the question asking respondents to rate the condition of the park they were visiting was good. A substantial number of respondents (19.3 percent) rated the parks as excellent, a large number (24.1 percent) rated the park's condition as fair, and only 12.6 percent rated the park's condition as poor. The park-specific breakdown on this question, however, indicates significant variation in response (see Exhibit 8.9). For example, New York's flagship, Central Park, as one might expect, received the highest rating of all parks maintained by the city. No one rated it fair or poor, and two-thirds of those interviewed in the park gave it a rating of excellent. No other park in which the survey was conducted was rated excellent by a majority of its visitors.

If we aggregate the data and use good and excellent as positive ratings and fair and poor as negative ratings, we see that eight of the ten parks in which we conducted interviews were perceived positively by users (see Exhibit 8.10). This included four parks—Central, Riverside, Prospect, and Fort Tryon—that were viewed positively by 75 percent or more of those interviewed. Two parks—St. Mary's and Jackie Robinson—were perceived negatively by a majority of the respondents interviewed in those parks.

Exhibit 8.9. Parks Rating: How Do You Rate the Quality of This Park?

Park	Excellent	Good	Fair	Poor	No Answer
Central	66.7%	33.3%	0%	0%	0%
Crotona	16.1	41.9	19.4	22.6	0
East River	10.0	50.0	22.0	14.0	4.0
Fort Tryon	33.3	42.1	21.1	3.5	0
Jackie Robinson	17.4	30.4	30.4	21.7	0
Morningside	6.3	68.8	12.5	12.5	0
Prospect	23.5	52.9	23.5	0	0
Riverside	12.5	83.3	0	4.2	0
St. Mary's	5.0	33.8	43.8	17.5	0
Sunset	13.0	43.5	26.1	17.4	0

Exhibit 8.10. Park Ratings Combined.

Park	Positive	Negative
Central	100%	0%
Crotona	58.0	42.0
East River	60.0	36.0
Fort Tryon	75.4	24.5
Jackie Robinson	47.8	52.1
Morningside	75.1	25.0
Prospect	76.4	23.5
Riverside	95.8	4.2
St. Mary's	38.8	61.3
Sunset	56.5	43.5

We also sought to measure the importance of parks to users and the intensity of citizen interest in the quality and maintenance of the city's parks. Exhibit 8.11 reports responses to the question, "How important are parks to you?" Nearly 75 percent of respondents said that parks were essential; only 2.4 percent stated that parks were not important. These results are similar to those reported in earlier studies.

The absence of variability in the response to this question, indicates that the meaning of *essential* may be imprecise. A more meaningful question might be the one posed regarding the amount of time a park user might be willing to volunteer to help improve the park. This question requires respondents to think of their own schedules and to envision a commitment of time and work. The results of our survey reflect that while nearly half of those questioned were unwilling to contribute time to improve the park, almost an equal number were willing to volunteer two hours per month. Nearly 10 percent of those interviewed said they were willing to contribute seven or more hours to park cleanup and maintenance on a monthly basis. Exhibit 8.12 reports the data drawn from this question.

Exhibit 8.11. How Important Are Parks to You?

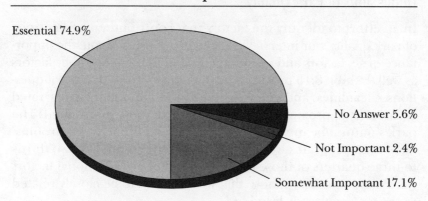

**Exhibit 8.12. How Much Time Are You Willing
to Contribute to This Park?**

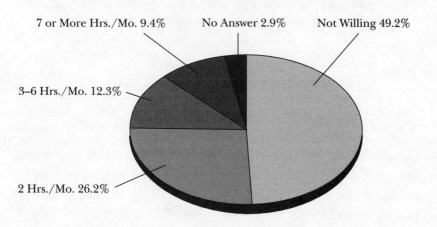

Dimensions of Park Quality

In an effort to identify the factors that contribute to perceptions of park quality, our interviewers asked park users to rate the importance of six factors and encouraged them to mention other factors as well. Exhibit 8.13 provides the data drawn from that set of questions. Cleanliness and safety were the most important factors, rated essential by approximately 85 percent of all those interviewed. The park's natural beauty, the repair of play equipment, bathrooms, and youth programs were also considered essential by two-thirds to three-quarters of those interviewed. Very few additional factors were mentioned, and those that were tended to be closely related to the factors already listed.

Use of Other Management Innovation Strategies

In addition to improving the way it monitors park conditions, the DPR has adopted a number of other innovative strategies to improve parks management (New York City Department of Parks and Recreation, 1996a). These include the following.

- *Managed competition.* The department has implemented two pilot projects to contract out parks cleanup and maintenance in ninety park facilities. The aim of this contracting effort is to reduce the costs of routine operations.

Exhibit 8.13. Park Quality Factors.

	Essential	Somewhat Important	Not Important	No Answer
Cleanliness	84.5%	10.7%	1.9%	2.9%
Safety	84.5	11.2	1.6	2.7
Natural Beauty	73.3	19.8	2.9	4.0
Play Equipment	67.1	16.0	12.0	4.8
Bathrooms	67.4	19.3	9.9	3.5
Youth Program	64.7	21.4	11.0	2.9

- *Increased computerization.* The DPR uses computer-assisted design in planning capital projects. As a result, the time involved in drafting designs has been reduced. The department computerized registration in all seven Manhattan recreation centers in 1996. DPR now issues all tennis permits through a computerized system, and plans to implement computerized registration in all of the city's recreation centers.
- *The use of workfare employees.* The DPR has been an aggressive and effective user of workfare labor. By the end of 1995 the department employed more than 3,600 participants in the city's employment program for welfare recipients, the Work Experience (or Workfare) Program. Their work has substantially improved the cleanliness of the parks during a time of budget cutbacks.
- *Public-private partnerships.* The department has made extensive use of volunteers and interns and has worked with a number of nongovernmental organizations in an effort to raise funds and cosponsor programs. A number of organizations have raised millions of dollars to support the parks, including the City Parks Foundation, the Central Park Conservancy, the Prospect Park Alliance, and the Riverside Park Fund.

Lessons Learned

The significance of this case is in part due to its portrayal of the impact of politics on management innovation. The DPR abandoned a promising effort to implement TQM due to changes in political leadership. TQM requires strong leadership and the personal commitment of key leaders. In government this can pose a challenge, because committed leaders are often voted out of office. Their successors tend to define themselves as an improvement on past leadership, which often leads the new administration to discard all visible legacies of the old guard. The average term of office of federal cabinet secretaries and city commissioners is significantly shorter than the five- to ten-year period required to institutionalize management reforms fully and integrate them into an organization's culture.

What can government innovators do to overcome this problem? First, innovators must attempt to make change agents out of nonelected, career officials. In the federal government, the career civil servants one would rely on would be the members of the Senior Executive Services and GS 13–15 officials. Unfortunately, New York City has no equivalent officials (Cohen and Eimicke, 1994b)—political allegiances run quite deeply throughout the city, and influence even first-level management staff.

Second, innovators should reduce the visibility of change efforts by dividing them into yearlong modules. This will lessen the probability that an incoming administration will feel the need to distinguish itself from the previous leadership by abandoning change efforts instituted by its predecessors.

In the case of New York City, or other places without sufficiently high-level permanent staff, innovators must move quickly and quietly. They must divide their efforts into self-contained yearlong modules. The innovation effort must be built on the assumption that it might be shut down rather quickly. We advocate slowing the pace of innovation in order to consolidate gains. Of course, the public manager must always remain aware that politics and public administration are intertwined and cannot be kept separate.

In retrospect, the DPR should have focused its efforts on a smaller number of organizational units, rather than trying to take the innovation departmentwide so quickly. Within those units, the DPR should have scaled back its aims to encompass only what it believed could be fully absorbed, reinforced, and internalized within a year. At the end of that year, it would have been able to assess next steps and tailor them to the individual unit.

Most efforts at management innovation do not take the case-by-case, micromanagement prospective we advocate here. Most commissioners are in a hurry, and seek large-scale macromanagement reforms that they can cite as success stories when building their own résumés. Selling management innovation techniques to an organization based on a slower but more surefooted approach will not be easy but may be the only way to ensure that innovations actually take root in highly politicized government settings.

A second lesson learned through the DPR case is that the demand for innovation is often externally driven. Budget reductions and increased customer demands drove both the Gotbaum and Stern innovation initiatives. Both commissioners spent substantial amounts of time raising private funds and forging public-private partnerships. Both employed welfare recipients to clean up parks. Both sought methods for enhancing performance with fewer resources.

Thus a negative external environment became the catalyst for internal efforts in management innovation. It was equally possible that cutbacks would have demoralized the department, and that resignation rather than innovation would have emerged. The question for students of management innovation, then, might be, Why did the parks department opt for innovation? There is no certain answer. To be sure, superior leadership played a role. Another contributing factor is that the services to which management innovations were applied were relatively straightforward; they did not include trying to end poverty or cure a persistent, fatal disease. As Commissioner Gotbaum often said, most parks operating resources are devoted to picking up garbage and litter and mowing lawns.

Parks services are relatively inexpensive but highly visible organizations. The utilization data presented earlier in this chapter indicate that it would be politically difficult to allow the parks system to deteriorate significantly. Nevertheless, it remains the case that a creative response to New York City's parks crisis of the late 1980s and 1990s was not a certain fate but rather a proactive choice by managers when faced with significant management challenges.

Chapter Nine

Innovation in Collaboration with Businesses and Nonprofits

The Indianapolis Private Industry Council

The city of Indianapolis has been innovating to improve its public services for nearly three decades, and its commitment to continuous innovation has paid off. Indianapolis is now the nation's twelfth largest city, with a thriving downtown. It is a center for transportation and distribution, conventions, and tourism; it is the home of one of the world's leading pharmaceutical companies; and it has an unemployment rate hovering around 3 percent.

Innovating as a Community Strategy: A History

In many respects, the commitment to continuous innovation began on January 1, 1970, when Indianapolis and surrounding Marion County merged to create one of the few metropolitan governments in the United States. Known as Unigov, the new structure consolidated many of the departments duplicated at the city and county levels. The mayor is elected countywide and is responsible for six major departments—public safety, metropolitan development, parks and recreation, transportation, public works, and administration. The city and county councils were also merged into a unicameral legislature, and a unified court system was established for the new jurisdiction.

Unigov was not created to deal with an impending crisis, such as municipal bankruptcy, or to avoid the consequences of a court order, such as desegregation or compliance with the one man, one vote rulings. Rather, the change was prompted by a good government reform movement seeking greater efficiency and effectiveness. The reforms were accomplished under (and largely through) the leadership of then Mayor (and subsequently U.S. senator and presidential candidate) Richard Lugar, who served from 1968 to 1975.

The changes helped Indianapolis to mitigate some of the tax base deterioration and suburban flight that accelerated the decline of other Midwestern cities during the 1970s and 1980s. Although the city faced strong economic competition from the Sun Belt and low-wage international producers, the post-Unigov Indianapolis was able to hold its own within the region and actually thrive as an urban area. A more efficient, less bureaucratic, and better bordered government contributed substantially to that economic survival.

Nevertheless, Indianapolis was at best economically stable throughout the 1970s. Fighting competition from inside and outside the region, the city was generally viewed as a weak sibling to Chicago and barely competitive with neighboring Cincinnati and Louisville. So, when William Hudnut became mayor in 1975, the central focus of his administration became the city's identity problem and its link to economic development. Hudnut's strategy proved to be popular and productive. He was elected four times (1974, 1979, 1983, and 1987) and served a total of sixteen years as mayor.

Hudnut sought to build the city's image and its economy through high-profile public projects and the aggressive pursuit of large corporate relocations and expansions. He was able to create enthusiasm and momentum around his development agenda by committing his administration to making Indianapolis the "amateur sports capital" of the United States. By his own account, Hudnut had a proactive philosophy of government, and he developed a public policy strategy that involved government in "attracting business and creating jobs" and "holding the downtown core" (Hudnut, 1995, p. xxxiii).

According to the *Boston Globe*, "The City was tired of being called India-no-place and Naptown and written off as a neon cornfield. . . .

So Indianapolis decided to become the amateur sports capital of America, built $168 million worth of facilities and [has] since brought in more than 250 national and international events" (Hudnut, 1995, p. 95). Although critics maintain he paid too much and left the city with too much debt, Hudnut also left the city with a much higher and better national profile, a claim to the amateur sports capital title, a real skyline, many new public facilities and amenities (including a National Football League franchise, the former Baltimore and now Indianapolis Colts), and a more vibrant economy.

Under Hudnut's watch, the RCA Dome (also known as the Hoosier Dome) was built downtown (and only subsequently attracted the Colts to play there); the adjacent Indiana Convention Center nearly doubled its exhibition space; and the abandoned, historic Union Station railroad terminal was converted into a retail mall and hotel complex. Other major projects developed and completed under Hudnut's leadership include the Sports Center, the Indiana University-Purdue University Natatorium, the Track and Field Stadium, the Major Taylor Velodrome, the renovation of the Indiana Repertory Theater, the Circle Theater, and expansions of the downtown White River State Park and the Indianapolis Zoo. Hudnut also used tax breaks and public investments to lure new employers to town, including United Airlines, Federal Express, and the U.S. Postal Service.

For Hudnut, the wisdom of his strategy all came together in the events of 1991. In April, the city hosted the National Collegiate Athletic Association's men's college basketball Final Four championship (which returned to the city in 1997), bringing sixty thousand visitors and $39 million in economic activity to the downtown stadium then known as the Hoosier Dome, and to hotels, restaurants, and shops. Later that year, the amateur sports capital hosted the World Gymnastics Championships, bringing participants from more than fifty countries to the former "brickyard in a cornfield."

In 1991, the U.S. Postal Service built a mail-sorting facility in Indianapolis, providing 750 new jobs. Later in the year, United Airlines selected Indianapolis as the site of a new $1 billion maintenance facility for its Boeing 737 fleet, creating 6,300 new permanent jobs. In both cases, the city's willingness to provide land, tax incentives, and low-cost, skilled labor helped win a national competition for the new facilities.

The Hudnut years exemplify the benefits and the costs of a public, capital-intensive economic development strategy. During Hudnut's sixteen years in office, more than thirty publicly assisted projects were undertaken in Indianapolis, requiring a city government investment of $436 million. That city investment leveraged nearly $600 million in state and federal dollars, $233.7 million from philanthropic sources (most notably the Lilly Endowment), and more than $1.5 billion from the private sector. There is little argument that the investments helped put the city on the national map, creating many employment opportunities in all three sectors; preserved and nurtured the city's downtown core; and made Indianapolis a major distribution and convention hub. At the same time, the city's capacity to spend additional public dollars, even for a solid return, was severely limited for the foreseeable future.

So, when Stephen Goldsmith ran for and was elected mayor of Indianapolis in 1991, he did not inherit a typical, decaying Rust Belt urban center that was past its prime. Nevertheless, the city was not without its problems. The downtown commercial revival had had minimal impact on inner-city residential communities, where housing, streets, sidewalks, sewers, street lights, and parks were generally in dire disrepair. Crime and crack were also prevalent in those neighborhoods, as well as unemployment at five to ten times the citywide average. Welfare rolls continued to increase while local businesses, large and small, were desperate for new workers.

Goldsmith's first campaign for mayor stressed economic competitiveness. In his view, the city's public policy for the previous decade had focused on making Indianapolis a more significant place. In large measure, that strategy centered on economic development, and the competition was Chicago, Cleveland, Detroit, St. Louis, and other Midwestern cities. Under Goldsmith (in his own words), "that concept continues, except increasingly our competition is our own suburbs" (Goldsmith, 1992, p. 2).

With the goal of making the city more competitive within and beyond the region, Goldsmith promised to reduce the size and cost of city government dramatically while improving what are generally characterized as public services (although increasingly these services may be delivered by nonprofit or private companies). During the 1991 campaign, the mayor frequently opined that in his view the city government could ultimately slim down to the mayor, a police chief, and four purchasing agents.

In many respects, that simple and exaggerated statement is very helpful in defining the deep differences and many similarities between the innovation strategies of Mayor Hudnut and Mayor Goldsmith. Unlike many Midwestern Republicans, Hudnut did not believe it was always true "that government is best which governs least. I had a proactive philosophy of government, not a caretaker one" (Hudnut, 1995, p. xxxiii). And as has already been discussed, Hudnut committed the city to spending public dollars for land, plans, strategies, facilities, and infrastructure, to attract businesses, create jobs, and hold the downtown core. The current healthy state of the Indianapolis economy is surely at least in some measure to his credit. Hudnut was also committed to improving neighborhoods and race relations, goals he had much less success in achieving.

Goldsmith came to the job of mayor with a vastly different background from his predecessor and with a similar vision but a very different set of strategies to achieve that vision. A lifelong resident of Indianapolis, Goldsmith graduated from Broad Ripple High School in 1964, received a bachelor of arts degree from Indiana's Wabash College in 1968, ventured to far-off Michigan to get his doctor of law degree with honors, and returned immediately after graduation to practice law in Indianapolis.

Goldsmith was drawn to public service through the law and the criminal justice system, serving successively as deputy corporation council, chief trial deputy, and ultimately eleven years as prosecuting attorney for Marion County. He gained a reputation as a tough law-and-order guy, but also as a person deeply concerned about families and children—about the importance of a rich family life for the future of society. He attracted national attention for his success in collecting child support for welfare moms, who he routinely referred to as his clients. This odd mix of accomplishments and images Goldsmith carried over to his administration as only the third mayor of Indianapolis since 1968.

Goldsmith stressed the need for smaller and more efficient government, and for a cap on city taxes, but he also committed his administration to providing safe streets, strong neighborhoods, a growing economy, and a greater voice for citizens in how their city is governed. At the core of his strategy for better government was a smaller, more focused government, and the first innovation tool he reached for was privatization.

Soon after taking office, Goldsmith set up a blue ribbon panel of business and community leaders to advise him on what city services should be privatized and how. That commission, called the Service, Efficiency and Lower Taxes for Indianapolis Commission, or SELTIC, is a council of ten people who Goldsmith calls "the most entrepreneurial business leaders in our community and 150 volunteers whose job is to go throughout government and identify transactions that can increase competition" (Goldsmith, 1992, p. 3).

The key word in Goldsmith's charge to SELTIC was *competition*. Very soon after his election, Goldsmith came to the conclusion that privatization had political limits and liabilities, and that private services were not necessarily better than the existing publicly provided version. In describing his strategy of competition, Goldsmith often begins by pointing out that private monopolies are only marginally more efficient than public monopolies. And that for public employees, the difference is a very big one, particularly if they are predestined to lose their jobs.

So Goldsmith and SELTIC shaped a privatization strategy to create a marketplace for municipal services. In their very first test of their innovation strategy, the filling of potholes, the mayor and his chief deputy on the project, Mitch Roob, faced a stern test from the municipal workers seeking to keep their jobs. The municipal drivers union came to Roob and the mayor contending that they had no fair chance of winning the bid because they had thirty-two supervisors for ninety-four drivers, appointed through the patronage of Goldsmith's Republican Party.

Goldsmith and Roob examined the situation and agreed with the assessment of the drivers, and Goldsmith gave notice to eighteen of his own party's political appointees. He remained committed to competition, even if there were very negative personal political consequences. The public employees submitted a bid and won the first contract for pothole repair.

During his first five years as mayor, Goldsmith has invited competition on both very large contracts—the operation of the airport and the wastewater treatment plant—and relatively small operations-mailroom services, microfilming, window washing, and messenger services. Overall, SELTIC has identified more than 150 opportunities to inject competition into the process of providing municipal services, and thus far Goldsmith has subjected more than sixty to the market test. The Goldsmith administration estimates that, on average, competitive bidding saves the taxpayer about 25 percent over the life of the contract, regardless of who wins the competition.

Through spring 1997, the city held more than sixty-four competitions for more than $500 million in work. The city workers won back all or part of twenty-nine contracts, and private firms won all or part of thirty-five, saving taxpayers more than $120 million over seven years. As a result of the competition, more than one thousand city positions were eliminated, a reduction in the workforce of about 20 percent. Yet only about two hundred people were actually laid off. Most of the former city employees went to work for the contractor who won the bid, shifted to other city positions, found related jobs, or took early retirement.

It is in this context of competition (privatization) and systematic rethinking of the way government conducts its business (strategic planning and reengineering) that Goldsmith sought to reinvent what was thought to be one of the national models of public job training and placement programs.

Rethinking Employment and Training: The Indianapolis Independence Initiative

Goldsmith's initiative to reinvent employment and training in Indianapolis began with his frustration that the economic boom in Indianapolis was not dramatically reducing poverty in the city. Throughout his first term in office, the cost of providing public services continued to drop, the economy continued to grow, the unemployment rate continued to drop, and yet the number of women and children receiving Aid for Families with Dependent Children (AFDC) remained high. By 1994, there were more than 15,000 AFDC families while local employers had 25,000 jobs they needed to fill. Though the comparison is by no means that simple, it still frustrated the mayor that he had been unable to use competition as effectively for social programs as he had for airports, wastewater, roads, and administrative services.

In addition, there were ominous signs on the economic development front. The mayor's staff involved in attracting new companies and facilitating corporate expansion in the city were coming back with as many explanations as proclamations. Indianapolis was not routinely winning the competition for new jobs anymore. Frequently the reason cited for choosing another site was the shortage of workers. This was particularly irritating to the mayor because the welfare rolls were quite high by historical standards and unemployment in most inner-city neighborhoods hovered near 20 percent.

The mayor knew that it would be more difficult to address the issues of long-term poverty and opportunity than it was to pave the streets, but he was committed to do what he could. He had found unconventional ways to alleviate poverty before in his public career, as Marion County prosecutor. He had increased child support payments from deadbeat dads to moms and children on public assistance in Marion County from $900,000 to more than $38 million by getting his staff to think of the moms and their kids as their clients and customers, by getting them to reengineer the enforcement procedures of the office. The mayor's commitment to reshape employment and economic support programs drew from that very successful and sustained child support initiative.

Mayors have very limited authority to redesign welfare programs on their own. In the early 1990s, when Goldsmith began his effort to reinvent the antipoverty strategy in Indianapolis, mayors had no control over welfare funds. So Goldsmith began his initiative with the related employment and training programs he could influence.

Similar to many other cities, Indianapolis had operated its employment and training programs directly out of the city government, specifically through the Division of Employment and Training within the mayor's Department of Administration. The division primarily received federal funds from the federal Job Training Partnership Act (JTPA), dispersed a good portion of the funds to the Indianapolis Private Industry Council (IPIC), and kept the remaining funds for staff and overhead functions such as planning, oversight, and accounting. The division also directed some

JTPA-funded, short-term, self-directed job-search programs, including work release from the county jail. In addition, they administered the funds for community-based multiservice centers, known as the Community Centers of Indianapolis, and for some youth and senior citizen programs.

Goldsmith was certain that these activities did not belong in his office, that they should not be thought of as administrative, and that they ultimately did not belong in government at all. He suspected that this administrative structure had simply evolved out of the old Comprehensive Employment and Training Act, or CETA program, the pre-JTPA federal program that simply subsidized government jobs for low-income individuals at the local level.

To begin the total rethinking of this effort, the mayor created the Office of Children and Family Services, transferred all the JTPA and community-based programs to it, and brought in an outsider, William B. Stephan, to develop a plan to make these programs work through competition, hopefully outside of government and with a strong base at the community level. This reengineering was done in the fashion that Hammer and Champy (1994) advocated in their earliest collaboration on reengineering—the mayor "just did it."

Stephan never expected to become known as a management innovator, particularly from the government side of employment and training services. He followed a circuitous path to his position as president and chief executive officer of the IPIC. Having grown up in a middle-class family in Indiana's second largest city, Gary (just outside of Chicago), Stephan sought out the warm weather and business administration expertise of Arizona State University for his undergraduate education.

A long-standing commitment to public service and a desire to work in all three sectors during his career led Stephan back to Indiana to complete a law degree at Indiana University School of Law-Indianapolis. Some internship, part-time, and administrative work during and shortly after graduation in the County Superior Court, Juvenile Division, eventually led to his appointment to the office of Magistrate of the Juvenile Division.

For six years, from 1986 through most of 1992, Stephan experienced firsthand the importance and difficulties of public administration, deciding cases involving juvenile delinquency, children in need of services, paternity, and related criminal cases. In addition to serving as judge and jury for cases of tragedy and futures at risk, he also handled the administrative responsibilities for the Division of Employment and Training staff of more than twenty professionals and support personnel. His performance in this difficult assignment convinced Mayor Goldsmith that Stephan could serve as family services coordinator, deputy director, and chief management strategist for the newly created Office of Youth and Family Services.

The mayor and Stephan reached the same set of conclusions regarding the future of employment and training in Indianapolis by the end of 1992 (only a few months after Stephan moved from County Court to his new position). Together they established a strategic plan with seven key principles around which their new workforce development program would be formed and implemented.

1. The traditional employment and training approach was much too narrow a construct. They needed and wanted a workforce development strategy.
2. Workforce development and economic development needed to be more closely linked. Increasingly, a skilled and affordable workforce was one of the key issues for businesses contemplating relocation to or expansion in Indianapolis.
3. Though the mayor needed to be very much involved in workforce development strategy development and policymaking, the staff supporting these initiatives did not need to be public employees.
4. Extensive national research conducted by the independent and widely respected Manpower Demonstration Research Corporation strongly suggested that workforce development programs should focus on rapid job attachment rather than on long-term education and training.
5. The mayor's competition model could work well in the workforce development areas, as demonstrated by a number of private and nonprofit firms in cities across the country that were effectively moving even long-term welfare recipients into self-supporting jobs using that approach.
6. The Office of Youth and Family Services was not the right place for the city's workforce development programs. To

demonstrate the importance of the program and link it to economic development, the mayor's office itself was a preferable but hopefully interim site. Ideally, the IPIC was the best place to locate workforce development policymaking and coordination. The IPIC is an independent, nonprofit organization created under the JTPA legislation, with a board comprised of the city's leading business CEOs, community-based economic development experts, and labor leaders (all appointed by the mayor).

Stephan and the mayor agreed that the IPIC needed to be restructured, to give up its role as the operator of the community's one-stop job centers and as the primary provider of federally funded employment and training services in the city (essentially referring one-stop customers to its own service-provider division). This would not be easy. The IPIC board and staff reflected the choices of former mayor Hudnut. Although Hudnut had left voluntarily, and although Goldsmith and he were both Republicans, it became apparent during Goldsmith's first year in office that the two had very different ideas about the proper role of government in the economy.

Hudnut was justifiably proud of his contribution to Indianapolis's emergence as a thriving American city. The IPIC was shaped by Hudnut's proactive vision of public economic development strategy. Unfortunately, Goldsmith's vision of the role the IPIC should play was very different. Not surprisingly, this created some obstacles in implementing the Goldsmith-Stephan strategy. A brief history of the IPIC should make clear the reasons that the obstacles developed.

The IPIC has evolved several times since it was incorporated as the Indianapolis Alliance for Jobs (IAJ) in 1979 under CETA. The IAJ initially helped the jobless move from publicly funded jobs into the private sector. The Reagan years brought a new philosophy of decentralization, local administration, and private sector involvement to the federally funded employment and training field. Embodied in the 1983 JTPA, the new law called for the establishment of local private industry councils composed of representatives from business, education, labor, and community organizations to administer local employment and training programs.

So, in 1983 the IAJ increased its membership to forty to meet the JTPA requirements, and Earl Harris, a well-known local business leader, took over as the chairman of both the IAJ and the new IPIC. The IAJ essentially became the service delivery division of the IPIC and, with the new JTPA funding the organization expanded its training capacity from less than two hundred to nearly six hundred persons annually. Throughout the 1980s, the IPIC continued to expand its service delivery to include the following:

- Partners 2000, a summer jobs placement program for disadvantaged teens, was launched in 1983, making youth employment an ongoing IPIC priority.
- Western Electric and RCA plant closures shocked the community, and shortly thereafter laid-off workers became another IPIC service priority.
- By 1984, the IPIC had become a major employment and training service provider, serving more than five thousand jobless adults and youth that year. Under a new chairman, Richard Kilborn, the council decided to get into a new business, adult literacy. Called UPwords, the program attracted corporate support from Blue Cross/Blue Shield and IBM, as well as national media attention. By the end of 1985, the IPIC had far eclipsed its IAJ origins, and the old organization and identity quickly faded away.
- In 1988, the difficult process of combining operations, facilities, personnel, and financial management for state public employment service and the nonprofit staff of the IPIC began.

The IPIC board and staff agreed that the evolution to an integrated employment and training system required a new image and public identity. After a full year of analysis, debate, discussion, and research, the organization officially adopted the Indianapolis Network for Employment and Training, or iNET, as its operating name and image in November 1989. IPIC and iNet are the same organization; iNet became the marketing name for IPIC just as Pepsi is the brand name for Pepsico. The name iNet illustrated a new philosophy of the one-stop shop. Under iNET, a wide range of programs (with different funding sources, rules and regulations, and eligibility requirements) would be provided to job seekers and employers by a combined staff of state and nonprofit employees from one central, downtown location and two satellite, one-stop centers (on the sprawling city's east and west sides).

By 1992, iNET was viewed by itself and many experts as a model in the publicly funded employment and training field. Its budget now exceeded $10 million annually from twenty-six different funding sources. For employers, iNET provided

- No-cost computer matching of job openings and job seekers for the city and surrounding counties
- Job applicant screening and assessment
- Specialized applicant recruiting assistance
- Labor market and wage information for human resource planning
- Central access to graduates from job training programs
- Technical and financial assistance to set up in-house training programs and hiring tax incentives
- Technical expertise on unemployment compensation and labor and employment regulations

For job seekers, iNET provided

- Free registration of skills and experience in the computerized job-match system
- A place to apply for unemployment insurance benefits
- Access to training, education, vocational programs, career counseling, and job placement
- Retraining assistance and financial aid for those whose skills were no longer in demand
- Preemployment assistance, including résumé preparation and training in job search and interviewing skills

iNET's approach reflected where the federal government thought employment and training should be focused. In 1992, the U.S. Department of Labor selected Indianapolis as one of thirty local programs (out of more than six hundred across the country) embodying the key components of President Bush's Job Training 2000 proposal.

In fall 1992, the mayor, Stephan, and iNET were of completely different minds regarding the state of employment and training efforts in Indianapolis. The iNET board and staff were basking in their recognition as a national model for the one-stop approach, and in their growing budget, larger staff, and many new product lines. The mayor and Stephan saw the city losing its competitive advantage as a business location and heard from prospective employers and their own economic development staff that the iNET approach simply was not working on the ground—the information and assistance they needed were not there when they needed them.

The employment training and placement system needed to be reengineered. This would not be easy. Although the mayor believed that iNET was a key component of an effective workforce development strategy, the organization needed to be radically changed at a time when it believed that it was the model by which others in the field should be measured.

Together, the mayor, Stephan, and others developed a multi-year plan (which changed somewhat along the way), based on a strategic plan, privatization and competition, a benchmarking effort, and a major reengineering effort. More than four years later, the city's workforce development has been completely redesigned and is again attracting national attention and recognition, but it remains a target for continuous improvement.

Reinventing Workforce Development

Before they fixed iNET, the mayor and Stephan decided they should do their homework. They sought an outside consultant who could look at the employment and training programs in the city, benchmark them against the rest of the country, and propose improvements. In January 1993, Eimicke began consulting work for the city and later for iNET.

This was not to be a long, drawn-out, descriptive study. Over four months, dozens of federal, state, and local government officials; employers large and small; iNET board members; and staff, customers, clients, and experts from the private, public, and nonprofit sectors were interviewed. The key points of Eimicke's report were as follows:

- iNET is indeed a national model for one-stop shops and voucher choice in employment and training, but its role as a direct service provider confuses its mission, creates questions and jealousy among other local service providers, and reduces its capacity as a broker of services.
- The city and iNET need to broaden their employment and training focus from worker preparedness and self-sufficiency to include an economic development focus on workforce planning and development, including labor market assessment, adjustment, recruitment, retention, and growth, in close cooperation with the public and private sectors. This new mission requires changes in the city's employment and training structure; in the relationship between the city and iNET; in the composition, responsibilities, and activities of the iNET board; and in iNET's relationship with its service providers.
- A reinvented iNET is an essential component and tool of the city's economic development strategy; therefore, responsibility for its policy direction and oversight should move to a new Office of Workforce Development, reporting directly to the mayor and focused solely on this new macromission.
- To move from service delivery to a broker and planning entity, iNET should spin off its service division as an independent nonprofit or for-profit company. After a transition year, the new entity would compete with other area service providers for contracts to operate the one-stop centers and to provide training and placement services.
- Because the reinvented iNET is the region's labor market and jobs expert, one of its key functions becomes providing individuals and corporate customers with meaningful scorecards on the performance of the area's education and training vendors, and redesigning its contracts with those vendors to emphasize outcome-based performance measures such as job placement, income enhancement, job retention, and advancement.

The report did not sit on a shelf. On the basis of progress reports submitted monthly, Stephan had advised the mayor on what were likely to be the key recommendations by early April. At the mayor's direction, Stephan began negotiating a new memorandum of agreement with iNET to redefine implementation of JTPA in Indianapolis for 1993 and beyond. On May 14, 1993, Joe Slash, chairman of iNET (and a former deputy mayor under Bill Hudnut), and Mayor Goldsmith signed the formal agreement establishing a partnership between iNET and the city for the implementation of JTPA and the provision of education, training, and employment services in the city.

Under the agreement, iNET became the administrative entity for Indianapolis and Marion County for JTPA, including the management and provision of education, employment, and training services. iNET also accepted responsibility for creating fair and open competition for selection of direct service providers. The agreement represented a major first step. The next step, development of a city-county employment plan, proved to be more difficult, controversial, and time-consuming than either Stephan or the mayor had anticipated.

The mayor's key objectives remained constant:

1. To make workforce development a full partner to economic development in the city's business recruitment and expansion efforts, mitigating businesses, fears that Indianapolis could no longer supply a sufficient number of skilled, affordable workers
2. To transform iNET from a service provider to a broker of services and planning-information agencies
3. To transfer to iNET as much of the city's workforce development efforts, staff, resources, and expenditures as possible.

By May 1994, these three principles and a twenty-four-month implementation plan were agreed to in detail by the city and iNET and formally approved by the iNET board.

iNET elected to begin the process of separating service delivery for policy and administrative support, and after a one-year transition, for its now-independent service delivery organization, thus opening up operation of the one-stop job centers and employment, training, and placement services to competitive bid. Simultaneously, the mayor announced the creation of the Division of Workforce Development, which reported directly to him, to supervise the transition, and he appointed Stephan as its head (the staff of the division consisted of Stephan and an administrative assistant).

With these two key decisions in place, the reengineering of iNET progressed rapidly. By July 1994, a restructuring task force and steering committee, composed of Stephan, key iNET board members, and Eimicke, submitted a ten-point reengineering plan to the iNET board and the mayor. The plan's final details were hammered out in a two-day strategic planning session attended by all board members who were able to attend, Stephan, Eimicke, and key iNET staff. The central points of the plan approved by the iNET board and the mayor were as follows:

1. iNET would become strictly a policy, planning, and systems management group on July 1, 1995. A new service delivery organization would be spun off from the current organization by July 1, and iNET would purchase those services from the new organization on a sole source, noncompetitive basis for one year. Thereafter, the service contract would be put out for competitive bid.
2. The new iNET board would have fewer members, who would have strong ties to other regional economic development efforts, and CEO-level participation would be emphasized.
3. An implementation-reengineering committee composed of five board members and five executive staff would be appointed to lead the effort and to report progress to the board, assisted by Eimicke and Stephan.

The iNET council accepted the plan virtually as proposed, except for the composition of the implementation-reengineering committee. Instead of five board members and five staff, the council appointed nine board members to the committee. To chair the reengineering committee and lead the effort, board chair Joe Slash chose Joel Yonover.

Yonover, an attorney from Chicago, was a strong advocate for the reengineering and reinvention of iNET, and was experienced in reengineering and entrepreneurship. He had a track record in taking over troubled and bankrupt high-risk insurance companies. He reengineered business lines, risk assessment practices, and financial systems, turning them around and making money.

Yonover took the second half of July and all of August to meet with key iNET staff, talk with iNET customers and clients, meet with board members and implementation committee members individually, and read everything he could acquire on the organization, its history, products and services, processes, funding sources, and legal restrictions and opportunities.

In September, Yonover sent a memorandum to the implementation committee members outlining what he believed would be the primary issues they would have to address. The key items on his list were

- Gaining approval from the state of Indiana to separate iNET into two organizations: IPIC and a service provider agency
- Determining the size and composition of the new IPIC board
- Ensuring availability of funds to complete the implementation and reengineering process
- Determining appropriate functions for the new IPIC and the service provider organization
- Establishing a framework for letting contracts and dealing with the associated liability issues
- Developing standards for judging contractor performance

In December 1994, the reengineering committee report was approved by the iNET board. The report specified the roles and responsibilities of the new IPIC and the service provider agency—seventeen functions for the new IPIC and twelve for the service provider agency. It called for standards for the sole source provider contract to be established by IPIC for the 1995–96 contract year, and for a Request for Proposal for competitive assessment of services in subsequent service years.

The report proved to be the blueprint for the reengineering effort, and most of the necessary actions occurred on or before the dates called for in the Yonover report. The board of the new service provider organization—called Workforce Investments, Inc., or WFI—met in late December 1994. By March 1995, existing iNET staff had been assigned to either IPIC or WFI or had moved on. Contract budget and performance issues were agreed to by April 1995, state approval for the sole source agreement was received in May, and in June 1995 the reengineering was completed and the two organizations began to function independently.

In May 1995, the new IPIC board and incoming chair Mike Alley (he was already on the board and knew he would be taking over July 1, 1995, well in advance of the meeting) met to set out a strategic plan for 1995–96. The organization had been through a great deal of change in 1994 and 1995, but in 1995–96 it would be a totally new organization, with a substantially new board and a completely redesigned mission.

The changes for IPIC were not quite over. Although IPIC's existing staff members never aggressively opposed the new strategic plan and the reengineering of IPIC's key business processes, they frequently voiced the concern that a national model for employment and training was perhaps being unnecessarily "improved." Many of the IPIC staff believed that IPIC was not at all broken. In fact, other private industry councils were copying its present form.

In October 1995, Alley and the new IPIC board appointed Stephan the new IPIC president. The mayor's Division of Workforce Development was immediately eliminated. IPIC was now the mayor's resource for workforce development information, expertise, planning, and implementation. The new team was quickly at the table when the city sought to recruit or retain industries, large and small.

At the mayor's request, IPIC played a major role in drafting the welfare reform plan for Marion County, as part of the state-mandated local welfare planning council initiative. With the help of a planning grant from the Rockefeller Foundation in spring 1994, IPIC and the mayor's office had been working for more than a year to use competition, rapid attachment to work, community-based organizations, and transition assistance to design a program that would make the welfare-to-work program a reality. The Local Welfare Planning Council established the slogan "work first" as the key to welfare reform and set out an essential role for the business community in developing career ladders, often across firms and even industries, so that new workers could move up from entry-level positions. Employers were also urged to devote additional resources to training to facilitate upward mobility in earnings and responsibility.

IPIC has continued to play a major role in the mayor's program to combat poverty and provide self-sustaining work for all those who are able to work. IPIC negotiated and administers a rapid job attachment contract with America Works, a private firm specializing in placing welfare recipients in jobs (profiled in Chapter Ten of this book). IPIC also staffed the 1996 Local Welfare Planning Council report, which presented a detailed proposal to the governor and the state legislature to permit interested localities to experiment with community-based, competitive welfare-to-work programs, as permitted under the new federal welfare reform law.

These new IPIC programs have involved the business community and neighborhoods in developing work-based initiatives to combat poverty and have earned Indianapolis

1. A federal Youth Fair Chance Center grant from the U.S. Department of Labor
2. An Enterprise Community designation and grant from Housing and Urban Development
3. A two-year grant from the Rockefeller and Mott Foundations to support welfare-to-work experiments
4. A grant from the Lilly Endowment to build transportation and support linkages from inner-city neighborhoods to jobs in the city's growing convention and visitors industries

IPIC also worked with the mayor to secure state legislative authority to use state and federal welfare dollars to support two comprehensive, neighborhood-based welfare-to-work pilots in Indianapolis.

In 1996, IPIC worked closely with the mayor to avoid the loss of $1 billion that would result from the closing of the Naval Air Warfare Center on the city's east side. The navy had planned to give the facility to the city and to relocate the workforce to other cities. Instead, the mayor, with IPIC's help, proposed a competition of private businesses to take over the facility and do the work for the navy at a lower cost. The president and Congress were ultimately sold on the idea, and the eventual winner of the competition, Hughes Technical Services, contracted to cut the navy's production costs by $225 million over five years (in addition to the $400 million in facility closing costs it was saving), to save the existing jobs, to add more than seven hundred jobs from other locations, to invest $7.5 million in capital improvements, to provide $500,000 for outplacement assistance (where necessary), and to invest 1 percent of its gross revenues in upgrading workers' skills. The city would also now receive taxes on what was a tax-exempt facility; it was repaid by Hughes for its costs in the privatization effort; and Hughes committed a second 1 percent of gross revenues for charitable grants and economic development in Indianapolis. This was indeed a new IPIC.

Early in 1996, IPIC moved forward on its commitment to open up to competition the operation of its one-stop career and job centers, the delivery of training and job-seeker assistance programs, and its automated client intake and case management data systems. By March 1996, eight proposals were received, including one from the current operator and former iNET division, WFI, and one from America Works.

Teams of IPIC staff, IPIC board members, and a representative of the state's workforce development staff participated in a rigorous evaluation and scoring process. Several proposals were deemed not fully responsive or not capable of meeting the contract requirements. The top three finalists—WFI, America Works, and Goodwill Industries—submitted outstanding proposals. Several staff and board members advocated awarding each organization the operation of one of IPIC's three major offices, but that posed major logistical and operational problems, and in any case the state representative indicated that the state would not approve such a plan. Ultimately, with much debate and some disagreement, the committee recommended and the IPIC board approved award of the new contract to Goodwill Industries.

The competitive experiment proved to be a great success. Goodwill Industries signed contracts with community-based organizations such as the John Bonner Center to open a new joint operation, the Career Corner, in the city's inner-city Near Eastside community. Goodwill was also very successful in building new paths to placements in the hospitality industry, and also in channeling clients with obstacles to employment (such as substance abuse) to appropriate treatment programs so they could become work-ready. America Works and WFI remain active and viable in the city and interested in pursuing new contracts when they come up for bid. The city, state, and IPIC were extraordinarily pleased with Goodwill's administration of the one-stop centers.

Alley and Stephan were satisfied that IPIC was now playing a major role in economic development and welfare reform, and they were gratified by the informal feedback they were receiving from the mayor and board members. But they were interested in a more comprehensive and detailed picture of what their customers were thinking. So, in January 1996 they commissioned a team of Columbia University faculty and graduate students in public administration to conduct a mail and telephone survey of IPIC customers and participating businesses.

The detailed survey of one hundred IPIC users (a mixture of job seekers and employers) provided some good news and some surprises. Just over half of the respondents expressed confidence in IPIC's ability to meet their employment-related needs, while only 17 percent were not confident about IPIC. The surprising aspect was that nearly 32 percent did not answer or answered that they did not know. Alley and Stephan were obviously pleased with the high favorable rating, but they were also concerned that such a high percentage of users were apparently either unaware of what services IPIC offered or were not using the services.

Some of the more detailed questions provided even more encouraging feedback that the strategic planning and reengineering innovations were responding to the needs of IPIC customers. Only 22 percent of the respondents indicated that IPIC could be most useful to them by providing access to job training (the "old IPIC"), while 51 percent indicated that IPIC could be most helpful in facilitating linkages to workforce suppliers. Another 44 percent responded that IPIC could be most helpful by providing customized labor market information. The top two program priorities of the strategic planning and reengineering efforts carried out by Alley and Stephan were also the top two priorities of IPIC customers and members.

Overall, the researchers concluded that the results indicated that the more experience a user has with IPIC, the more confident they become that IPIC can effectively serve their workforce development needs. The researchers therefore concluded that IPIC needed to focus more on communication with its members, the business community at large, and job seekers to get the word out about what IPIC could do for employers and potential employees. Communication became a top priority of IPIC's 1997 strategic plan.

Learning Through Innovation

Mayor Goldsmith and his top staff have been making management innovation work since 1991. Their success illustrates that innovative management techniques are not just for times of crisis or turnaround situations. Goldsmith inherited a healthy, well-run city and innovated to make it even better.

The Goldsmith team has also learned through innovation. Starting out as virtual privatization ideologues, they rather rapidly rejected privatization as an all-purpose cure. Competition has certainly become a pervasive technique in the Goldsmith regime, but it is usually supplemented or taken a step further using reengineering, strategic planning, and benchmarking. In all cases, Goldsmith and his key deputies ground their innovations in carefully constructed and periodically revised strategic plans.

Goldsmith himself regularly borrows from the TQM toolbox. Customer-citizens are surveyed often to find out what services they desire and how they define quality in those service areas. Permitting public employees to compete with private contractors has not only improved the efficiency of the public sector in Indianapolis, it has also led to the increasing use of team management by public agencies. Finally, Goldsmith's overall management philosophy reflects his belief that continuous improvement is necessary and possible.

The Goldsmith administration has learned a great deal about the benefits and limits of privatization, strategic planning, and reengineering over the past six years. Regarding privatization, the mayor quickly learned that he really was not an advocate of privatization at all—what he really wanted was competition to produce the best possible public services at the lowest possible prices. As he and his people attempted to bring competition into the provision of public services, they learned that it was not going to be as easy as they had thought.

First, they learned that their existing accounting system was incapable of telling them how much it was currently costing to fill a pothole, wash a window, or deliver a package. A substantial amount of time and effort was devoted to creating an activity-based cost accounting system so that the city could effectively compare its current unit costs with bids from other potential service providers. In the case of pothole repair, the mayor learned that unnecessary patronage management positions filled by his party's loyal lieutenants would make it impossible for current public employees to compete fairly for the new, bid contracts. The mayor eliminated the unnecessary positions and ultimately the public employees won the pothole contract. The public benefited by receiving even better services at a lower cost. Public employees saved their own jobs and gained respect for a mayor they were convinced they would hate. The mayor had the satisfaction of knowing that his innovative tools were working, although he had incurred the cost of alienating his own party, which some argue later cost him the election for governor.

The wastewater treatment plant, airport, employment and training, and Naval Air Warfare Center privatization competitions were all generally big wins for Indianapolis and the mayor. Big savings, major service improvements, more jobs, and a healthier economy resulted. But even these big wins had bumps and blemishes—charges of unnecessary fish kills caused by the wastewater operator, resentment by local businesses when outsiders such as America Works won contracts in the city, public employee unrest when they did not win the competition, and the inevitable innuendo from the losers that political influence was the real deciding factor in the contract award process.

Not all of the competitions produced substantial savings, and sometimes job losses occurred. Creating a playing field that enables small businesses and community-based organizations to compete effectively remains a challenge. The use of outside consultants, including national firms and university experts from outside the state, is usually politically unpopular.

Overall, the Indianapolis experience with privatization as a tool has been positive because they have done it with care. They spent the time to develop a unit cost–based accounting system. They decided to enable public employees to compete and stay competitive through training. The mayor has also toned down his rhetoric since the 1991 campaign. For example, he no longer talks of reducing the city government to himself, the police chief, and four purchasing agents.

The mayor kept the core functions in government and worked to improve public services using other innovation tools. He has considered short- and long-term consequences when assessing the advisability of privatization, and has used a variety of contract terms, leases, and sales and participation arrangements where appropriate. Strategic planning has been the foundation for all the other innovations that the Goldsmith administration has used over the past six years. Often praised as a bright, independent, and thoughtful leader, Mayor Goldsmith is sometimes criticized for being too insular, for revealing new directions full-blown and implementing them with little time for input, discussion, debate, modification, and consensus building. A commitment to strategic planning has helped the mayor to curb these tendencies, to come up with even better strategies, and to implement them with less difficulty, having built awareness and support during the planning process.

The use of strategic planning has enhanced the mayor's reputation for leadership, comprehensive viewpoint, and capacity for bringing all segments of the community together to achieve common objectives. A small but significant illustration of how strategic planning works for Indianapolis is their success in attracting and hosting the men's college basketball Final Four competition in 1991 (in the midst of what was a downtownwide construction site), getting the prestigious event back in 1997, and a contract to host it again in 2000.

Strategic planning has not been without costs for the mayor and his administration. Strategic planning takes time and money. It has slowed the mayor down at times and has required him and his deputies to spend a great deal more time than they would like seeking foundation and corporate support to pay for the research and consultants that serious strategic planning requires.

Strategic planning involves making some choices explicit, and that aspect has fueled the mayor's critics. A strategic planning assessment of welfare policy in the city and state led the mayor to conclude that the existing system should be blown up and replaced with a privatized, work-based system that enables and empowers poor people. Though many outside observers have identified Goldsmith's Indianapolis Independence Initiative as a national model, the trade-offs that the plan made explicit earned the mayor the active opposition of the welfare establishment during his 1996 unsuccessful run for governor and have made it very difficult for him to get the required state approvals to go forward with the plan from the state welfare administration that Goldsmith vowed to blow up.

Reengineering has worked in Indianapolis, producing the promised dramatic improvements in its workforce development and employment and training programs. IPIC is now the community's recognized authority and resource for workforce development policy and information. Companies such as America Works, The Training Institute, and Goodwill Industries provide employers and employees with a choice of job training and placement services, and payment is predominately based on performance, not process. Community-based organizations are linking to IPIC and these placement firms through contract-based relationships and through an Internet-based information-sharing network that is already being tested in the city's near-Eastside neighborhood.

Reengineering also has its costs, however. The reinvention of IPIC took more than four years and would not have been possible were it not for grants from the Rockefeller Foundation. Foundation grants were critical to IPIC's continued involvement in the welfare-to-work reforms and to keeping a broad range of job placement firms active in the city. If the state gives the city flexibility to use its share of federal welfare dollars creatively, the new initiatives will continue after the grant funds run out. If not, it will be difficult for IPIC to sustain the integrated employment and training provider network of community organizations and private companies it has developed.

Positions have been eliminated from the Office of Youth and Family Services, the mayor's office, and IPIC. WRI lost its contract to operate the one-stop centers and has downsized as it seeks new contracts, primarily in program evaluations and audits of other employment and training providers. To our knowledge, everyone who was previously employed in the old system is working and the net number of persons employed in Indianapolis has increased substantially during the Goldsmith years. However, not everyone was pleased with losing his or her job, nor is everyone happy with his or her new employment. Disruptions and dislocation are part of reengineering, and Goldsmith and Stephan have made some enemies as part of the innovation process.

The mayor was reelected in 1995 and was not elected governor in 1996. As a result, he and the chief architects of the various competition, strategic planning, and reengineering initiatives have stayed around and sustained the innovations well into the implementation phase. Had Goldsmith lost his bid for reelection as mayor or won for governor, one or more of the innovations may have floundered or may have been deliberately abandoned, as Betsy Gotbaum's TQM program was in the New York City Department of Parks and Recreation.

Chapter Ten

America Works

A Private Company Carrying Out a Public Service

America Works is a relatively new, entrepreneurial company with its roots in the 1960s commitment to fighting poverty, but its growth and success come out of the government privatization movement of the 1980s and 1990s. The company is the creation of its founder, Peter Cove, and its CEO, his wife, Lee Bowes. America Works is in the business of finding sustaining jobs for people on welfare and keeping them there, in return for a placement and retention payment from government.

Cove, who refers to himself as a social activist and businessman, in that order, believes that private sector jobs are the most effective weapon against poverty. But Cove came to his current position and philosophy through a three-decade career in the public, nonprofit, and private sectors that was unified by his overarching commitment to help people help themselves. A graduate of Northeastern University with a degree in sociology, Cove began his professional odyssey in the mid-1960s in the New York City government bureaucracy. Frustrated by government's slow-moving, hierarchical chain of command and by plans constantly disrupted by elections, Cove migrated to the nonprofit sector, seeking social reformers as dedicated as himself who viewed work as a potent weapon against poverty and urban decay.

He worked in several foundation-funded community employment, civil rights, and education programs before landing in what would become his life's work—helping poor people get the skills

171

they need as quickly as possible so they can land a job that supports themselves and their families. His first career step in that direction was as director of the Manhattan Project in New York City for Wildcat Service Corporation, a government- and foundation-funded program to help the hard-core unemployed turn their lives around through skill-building work.

The Wildcat position led Cove into what would be the first stage in the development of his breakthrough philosophy, the presidency of Transitional Employment Enterprises (TEE), a nonprofit job placement operation funded in part by the Ford Foundation. Cove served as president of TEE for eight years, from 1976 to 1983. It was there that he experimented with various methods of using support mechanisms and limited, applied training techniques to move what were believed to be the disadvantaged and hard-to-employ into self-sustaining private sector work.

At TEE, Cove developed and refined his belief that work was central to a person's life. His experiences there convinced him that work was essential for most people, not just as a source of income but also to provide a definition of self, a measure of self-worth, and a role in something bigger than oneself, and as a mode of therapy; he also saw that people on public assistance wanted to work as much or even more than anyone else. The TEE experience was also important because it was there that he forged his professional and personal bond with Lee Bowes.

While a graduate student at Columbia University's School of Social Work in the mid-1970s, Bowes independently reached the same conclusion as Cove: that work should be the foundation of any serious antipoverty strategy. After completing her work at Columbia, Bowes ran a large, federally funded public jobs program under the old Comprehensive Employment and Training Act, or CETA, as it was more generally known.

Bowes was quite effective as a CETA manager, placing more than two thousand previously unemployed people in local government jobs. Despite her success and the immediate benefits to her customer–job seekers, Bowes was not sold on the long-term viability of the CETA concept. In her view, the administrative costs of the effort were extraordinarily high. The jobs for the CETA job seekers were often little more than make-work or fill-in positions.

There was poor supervision, little or no training, and virtually no career ladder. Working was better than not working, a paycheck was better than a handout, and a CETA network was better than no network to the next job; but Bowes became convinced that market-driven jobs in the private sector were a more viable antipoverty strategy.

In 1978, the opportunity to test her new theory came along with a job offer at TEE. The TEE experience fundamentally changed Bowes's life. During her nine years at TEE (she stayed three years after Cove left to start America Works in 1984), Bowes became sold on the private sector jobs model, received her Ph.D. from Boston University in unemployment and social policy, and developed the design that was to become America Works.

TEE was established by the Ford Foundation and the Manpower Demonstration Research Corporation. At its core, the organization was nonprofit, experimental, and dedicated to learning. Both Bowes and Cove learned a great deal at TEE about what does and does not work in getting those with minimal experience and skills from dependency to work.

Bowes and Cove came to believe that the persistent concerns about "creaming" in employment and training programs were misplaced. Essentially, the creaming theory is that without random assignment of customers, employment and training firms will target the best and the brightest of the unemployed, place them in jobs that they would have found on their own, and then rip off government and/or foundations for a placement fee they did not really earn. At the same time, the employment and training firms will systematically shun and discourage the low-skilled, hard-to-place customer, moving on to a new location once the cream is gone.

TEE served primarily difficult-to-place customers. Dealing with job seekers face-to-face, day after day, for more than a decade, Bowes and Cove became convinced that the cream could not be easily labeled. Those with the most skills at the outset and those who were the most well adjusted or the most experienced were not necessarily the customers easiest to place or the most likely to be retained and to move up and out of dependency. Attitude was extremely important. So was dressing, talking, and acting for success, and being on time, seeking out opportunities, and knowing how to plan and prioritize assignments. On the ground, formal education and experience were not as important as attitude, energy, perseverance, and a willingness to learn the employer's way.

TEE was not an employment agency. Rather, it was in business to serve the hard-core unemployed and those who were difficult to place. Bowes, in fact, expanded the business to the elderly, the mentally ill, the mentally retarded, and the physically challenged.

The nature of TEE's customers also helped Bowes and Cove debunk another commonly held belief—that the welfare population and hard-core unemployed do not want to work. Day by day, person by person, for nearly a decade, Bowes and Cove experienced the reality that those without jobs generally want to work as much as or even more than the average working person. These people are not working and have not worked for long periods of time not only because they lack skills but, perhaps more important, because they have no networks to jobs and do not know basic workplace behaviors, even if they are lucky enough to identify a viable job opening.

The building blocks of what were to become the America Works formula were taking shape.

- Real jobs with a future were a better antidote to poverty than make-work jobs created for the sole purpose of generating income.
- The biggest obstacle to work for the unemployed was no access to a network. At TEE, Bowes and Cove learned that most jobs come through a network, not through the newspaper. Middle- and upper-class workers find jobs and move up the ladder based on contacts and performance, in that order. No matter how good you are, no matter how impressive your résumé, you cannot get the job if you do not get in the door.
- Employment and training programs were much too focused on long-term training and on education with little connection to what jobs were available in the marketplace and what was required to get those jobs. Rapid job attachment, help in overcoming obstacles in the early months of work, and on-the-job training seemed to be more effective in getting jobs for hard-to-place job seekers and keeping them employed.

- Attitude, energy, and appropriate work behaviors were as important as experience and skills, particularly for entry-level positions and the first few steps up the career ladder.

By 1984, Cove was ready to test his theories as an entrepreneur. An improving national economy, the Reagan administration's drive to shrink government and to privatize many of its functions, and a growing public frustration with rising welfare costs convinced Cove that there was a market for a business that could move welfare recipients into existing private sector jobs.

With $1 million in savings and bank loans, Cove set off to launch America Works in 1984. He based his decision to leave TEE on three factors. First, he wanted to prove that his theories about rapid job attachment could work anywhere. Expansion required new capital, and he did not believe that a nonprofit was a viable vehicle to attract venture capital. Second, he wanted to make more money for himself and that was difficult in a nonprofit, research setting. Third, he thought that the discipline of a for-profit structure would maximize the efficiency of the operation, and thereby the profit for himself (Rothman and Scott, 1992).

America Works's initial project was not successful. Its first client, the state of Ohio, came to Cove because of the positive publicity and word of mouth about his work at TEE in Boston. The governor of Ohio basically forced the social service bureaucracy into testing the America Works concept. The theory proved to be valid, and America Works was able to move welfare recipients into private sector jobs rather quickly and keep them there. Unfortunately, the process of getting started was handled poorly, and within two years Cove was forced to shut down the Ohio operation.

The governor of Ohio believed that work was better than welfare and that a privatized approach to combating welfare was a good way to accomplish that objective. Neither the governor nor Cove took the time to sell the state's welfare department on the idea. Because the welfare department administered the contract, made the payments, and would ultimately evaluate its success, the failure to bring them along from the beginning proved to be a fatal mistake. The officials at the department also did not like the fact that America Works was from outside the state, and its for-profit structure seemed unseemly to some who thought it unethical to make money off the poor or to divert funds intended for the poor to performance payments to America Works (Rothman and Scott, 1992). Speaker of the House Thomas P. O'Neill's guiding principle that all politics are local was a lesson that Cove was reminded of immediately, and he would encounter the issue again in future projects.

Connecticut was America Works's first success story and the local political climate contributed to a much better experience for all concerned. The state had already begun to experiment with welfare-to-work initiatives, and they came to TEE and Cove in 1984 as part of an informal benchmarking exercise.

This time, it was not the governor forcing the experiment. Several key state officials and the welfare commissioner were part of a team of policymakers that invited America Works to come to Hartford. From the beginning and over time, America Works built support among legislators, the welfare department executives and staff, the governor's office, the press, auditors, the media, the public, and most important, its employer and its job-seeking customers.

By the early 1990s, America Works was moving 150 welfare recipients from public assistance to self-sustaining work each year and had encouraged several competitors to get into the business. Welfare-to-work in Connecticut had evolved from a radical, narrowly supported idea to a popular policy in less than a decade, in part due to the success of America Works. By 1987, America Works was enough of a business to require more capital and a full-time chief executive officer.

Bowes and Cove decided to tie their entire professional and financial future to America Works, and Bowes joined the company as chief executive officer. At that time, Bowes and Cove met Abe Levoitz, a successful manufacturer who had recently retired and was looking for new challenges. Levoitz became the third member of the leadership team, providing a reliable source of capital and the business savvy and experience that Cove, the visionary, and Bowes, an operations specialist, lacked. The key ingredients were now in place. Within a year, America Works was in New York, perhaps the most challenging location for a welfare-to-work initiative.

In 1988, America Works was invited into the state by the Cuomo administration to rescue a state-funded welfare-to-work experiment that was failing. Again, the politics were right; the state had already reached internal consensus that the idea was worth experimenting with and began with a local company. America Works came in by invitation to save the local experiment, and the state social services commissioner was one of the key policymakers who chose America Works to come into the state.

By 1996, America Works was operating in New York City, Albany, and Indianapolis, and was in serious negotiations with Baltimore (which signed on with America Works in 1997), Philadelphia, and several cities in Florida. Since its inception, America Works's formula had been praised in the media several times, both domestically and internationally. In addition, Cove and Bowes were now invited regularly to testify before congressional committees.

With national welfare reform legislation signed into law in 1996 and jobs-based solutions to poverty attracting liberal and conservative support, the time seemed right for the expansion and growth of America Works (Cohen and Eimicke, 1997). However, in the most mature of the existing offices, New York City, Bowes noticed signs that the organization was not in perfect health. Job placement rates had plateaued, staff attrition rates were higher than historic norms, and negative static on the office grapevine was clearly audible, even to the boss.

Organizational Obstacles to Entrepreneurial Growth

Bowes and Cove had long believed that the secret of their continued success was their strong, diverse, highly motivated, and caring staff. By spring 1996, the New York City office staff was sounding and more frequently acting like a regular business. To Bowes, such sounds were ominous.

Bowes had the final say on all hires and she exercised that responsibility in a very active manner. She always looked beyond the experience and past performance of a prospective employee to find people who would be happy each morning to head into America Works and who would be inspired by each successful placement—people who would be happy helping individuals and families to turn their lives around. Bowes now sensed that the joy and inspiration were being displaced by frustration and unhappiness. Despite her position and hands-on style, it was difficult for Bowes to find out directly what was going wrong.

To begin to figure out the problem, Bowes called in Richard Greenwald, who holds the title of development director. While his job description calls for him to work primarily on finding new cities for the company to operate in, America Works's horizontal structure and entrepreneurial, small-business roots meant that Greenwald actually handled a wide variety of tasks, ranging from the staffing and start-up of the Indianapolis office to writing speeches, doing advance work, developing policy papers, setting up an office information system, making presentations to business groups, and dealing with vendors. Along with Bowes, Greenwald was also in-house management analysis expert.

Greenwald started his career in the public sector, with stints as legislative analyst in the office of then U.S. Senator Al Gore and later in the U.S. Environmental Protection Agency. He deepened his knowledge of and interest in management innovation in Columbia University's Master of Public Administration program. There, Greenwald developed a strong belief in the potential value of TQM and team management.

Bowes and Greenwald concluded that they wanted an outside perspective and some additional expertise in management innovation. They decided to call us in to do an assessment of their organizational structure and to determine what innovations might work best for them. Bowes had used Eimicke before—to document and assess the organization's basic curriculum and to help staff and organize the new offices in Indianapolis and Albany. Following several daylong visits to the New York City office, interviewing staff and observing operations, and detailed discussions with Bowes and Greenwald, we recommended a pilot project to test team management as a method of improving morale and increasing productivity.

A number of significant obstacles to more efficient operation of the New York City office related to organization structure.

1. Placing and retaining welfare recipients in permanent jobs are extraordinarily complex and difficult tasks that require the participation of virtually every unit of the America Works operation, yet there was no structural mechanism to coordinate the various units to act in a timely fashion other than a direct order from Bowes herself.

2. A recently updated compensation and bonus system rewarded only individual performance. There were no financial incentives for cooperation or coordination, which are essential to virtually every successful placement.

3. While most staff appreciated the absence of hierarchy and bureaucracy at America Works, many also expressed frustration with a frequent inability to get things done. Several staff members articulated a "hunger for management."

4. The horizontal structure left it unclear to most staff what opportunities for career advancement were at America Works. Most employees were interested in staying at America Works and found the prospects for more money pleasing, but they were also interested in enhancing their résumés. It was not apparent to anyone how to advance your career by staying with America Works.

5. To most employees, the only way to make real income gains at America Works was to be in the sales unit. This unit is responsible for identifying new job openings with participating employers. Staff members assigned to other units were also important in generating profit, but received less compensation.

6. The key step in a successful placement was the job match unit. Yet, with only one person doing that function, it was also the biggest bottleneck in the organization.

7. Everyone complained of serious backlogs in the accounting and payment unit, in terms of getting vendors paid, receiving reimbursements and bonuses, and even getting information regarding the status of a payment order.

8. The office information system was a mess. The reception system was unreliable, there was no voice mail, and there was no effective way to reach someone who was away from his or her desk. This was an obstacle and presented a poor image to potential customers.

Innovation Attempted

Based on the obstacles identified and the nature of the America Works organization and corporate culture, we recommended a pilot test of team management in the New York City office. Bowes selected the members: a senior and junior salesperson, a corporate representative—the person who assists the candidate through their six-month trial period on the job—the job-match person, and someone from accounting or finance. She also designated Richard Greenwald as project coordinator, to serve as the key link between Bowes, the team and its members, and the consultants.

We met with the pilot team members collectively and individually to get some sense of how they currently worked together, the obstacles they faced, and some of their initial impressions of how teams might work best at America Works. We then designed a team management guide and handbook for America Works, drawing on its previous work with other organizations as well as key resources from experts in the field. We also requested, and America Works agreed to purchase, copies of the second edition of *The Team Handbook,* edited by Peter Scholtes (1996), for the team members and top management. Participants were also urged to read Jon Katzenbach and Douglas K. Smith's *The Wisdom of Teams* (1993). Included in the America Works Team Guide were definitions of team and team management; material on team formation, team operation and management, and teams and career paths; and a team troubleshooting guide.

The guide was reviewed and approved by Greenwald and Bowes in early June 1996. It was then time to develop a training and implementation schedule. Given the organization's historically slow work flow in June and July, America Works decided that the team would officially kick off its work on August 1, 1996, and work for a sixty-day pilot-test period that would end on September 30, 1996. During July and August, Bowes, Greenwald, and the team worked with us to develop a series of measures to assess the performance of the team, considering such possibilities as increased job orders, higher efficiency of candidate hiring (ratio of candidates sent to hires), higher retention rates, employee morale, and efficiency of office operations.

Training sessions were held for team members in July. The sessions focused on the basics of team management, how their team would operate, the schedule for the next several months, and dealing with problems as they arise. Separate team leader training sessions were held in July for Greenwald and the first America Works team leader, Phil Jones. These sessions focused on the basics of being a team leader, covering such topics as the role of the team leader and its members, how to run a team, the tools of work analysis, identifying improvement needs, the stages of process improvement, and team dynamics and team-building exercises. The team also worked on some ideas for developing a performance-based bonus contract with management.

The selection of Phil Jones as the first team leader proved to be critical to the success of the team management. Phil Jones was a star performer at America Works. He joined the organization through its Hartford, Connecticut, office in 1987 and moved to the New York office and headquarters in 1988.

Though his title was marketing director, Jones was known as a salesman without peer, the best in the office, for as long as anyone could remember. Of course, at America Works sales has a bit of a different meaning than in most organizations. At America Works, a sale means finding an employer willing to hire someone who is currently on welfare for a permanent job that has the potential to pay a salary with benefits sufficient to get that individual and their family off the welfare roles. For America Works to get paid for the "sale," the individual placed must complete a six-month probation period. During his first decade at America Works, Jones was directly involved in helping more than three thousand welfare recipients move from dependency to self-sustaining work. In his free time, Jones cared for his sister and challenged kids, served as president of his church choir, and was financial secretary to its board and an adviser for the youth ministry.

As America Works expanded, Bowes hoped that Jones would become primarily a manager, either running a new city office or serving as a senior manager in the headquarters of a much larger America Works of the future. Both Jones and Bowes were less than pleased with his previous execution of management functions. The hope and expectation was that Jones's reputation would inspire the team members and that a positive team leader experience would jump-start his management career.

The team met regularly during the second half of July and throughout August. As the busy fall quarter began, Jones was excited, motivated, and functioning effectively as a team leader. He was becoming an effective manager, acquiring a much better sense of how to bring people out, balance contributions to meetings, and build consensus for group decisions.

The team had developed a sense of mutual interdependence and a new appreciation of the interconnectedness of their collective and individual success. Though all of the team's work was ultimately tied back to the bottom line of higher revenues for the company, all of the participants reported that a renewed sense of the motivational factors brought them to America Works in the first place. Jones, Greenwald, and the other team members also reported that they were managing meetings and their time much more effectively as a result of the team training and team experience. Team activities and regular work were rapidly merging, as participants came to see that the work of the team and their individual assignments were very much complementary parts of the same whole.

Once during the fall, a team meeting was canceled to address the "crisis of the day," raising serious concerns among team members. When Jones was able to explain that the crisis was real and the cancellation unavoidable, the team was reassured. At the same time, Bowes was also learning that team management had become serious business in the New York office and the old entrepreneurial ways of operating "on the fly" would have to change from her side of the equation as well.

What had begun as a small experiment was taking on much more significance. Bowes had expected a verbal report of a couple of ideas from Jones or at most a two-page memo from Greenwald with a couple of ideas from the team early in September. Instead, the team worked through September, October, and into November, producing a twenty-page draft report with two major appendixes just before Thanksgiving.

The key issue that the team could not resolve, even by Thanksgiving, was how to reward members of the team fairly for improved performance, assuming that they could reach agreement with management on how performance should be measured and on the appropriate formula for computing bonuses for the sales staff. The salespeople, including Jones, were not very enthusiastic about giving up some of their increased bonus potential just as the new formula was going into effect.

Following another month of discussion and polishing, the group named itself Team USA and submitted its report, "The New

Beginning for America Works: A Vision for the Future," in December 1996. The report's key recommendations were organized into three categories: changes in operational behavior, cost analysis, and performance incentives. Recommendations for changes in operational behavior included creating a formal schedule for the job match coordinator's diverse activities, training sales staff to conduct better mock job interviews, enforcing more rigorously the attendance policy for candidates still at America Works, involving corporate representatives in sales activities, and increasing the number of opportunities for communication between staff and top management. The report's cost analysis findings reflected that the vast majority of the team's recommendations could be implemented at little or no cost. Items of notable cost that the team recommended included the hiring of a college intern, the purchase of a new copier, more detailed market research, a more aggressive advertising campaign, and the purchase and implementation of a voice mail system.

Bowes was extremely impressed with the report's scope, detail, and number of no-cost and low-cost improvements. She had thought that team management would improve operations and reinvigorate the staff, but she never expected such a substantial increase in enthusiasm and effort. Dozens of the small but important suggested improvements were put into place immediately. The broader recommendations required some thought, time to implement, and resolution of the difficult issue of performance incentives.

The most difficult part of America Works's move into team management was creating financial incentives that rewarded team performance. All of the financial incentives at America Works were individual-based and heavily oriented toward the sales (job vacancy and placement) staff. The fact that the organization had just paid for an outside consultant compensation study and implemented a new bonus plan for the sales staff made the new team incentive proposal even more difficult to implement.

Team USA's analysis and proposal was quite simple. An average cumulative monthly billings history was developed for the team members. The team projected that implementation of its low- or no-cost operational improvements and more efficient team approach would result in a consistent 3 percent increase over the normal monthly billings for the team's members, and it requested that management split the incremental gain with the team 50-50. Despite a wide range in base salary and totally different bonus plans, the team members would split their share of the bonus evenly—everyone would get exactly the same amount.

Bowes was intrigued and persuaded, but a little cautious. Changing the entire compensation plan, even for nine employees, would have broad consequences in New York, Indianapolis, and Albany, as well as in future sites, particularly if it worked. Bowes had to be sure that the methodology was sound, that true costs were reflected, that provisions were made for changes in the external environment, and that the baseline was accurate. In March 1997, Team USA's plan went into operation, although the new team performance incentive plan was not implemented.

Nevertheless, the results were dramatic. During 1996, the team members had averaged fifty-seven placements per month, with March the second lowest month of the year. In March 1997, Team USA made ninety-three placements, an increase of more than 60 percent. Although she had no expectation that such extraordinary gains could be maintained, Bowes was so impressed with the initial results that she decided to start two additional teams in the New York City office. In addition, a new contract for the city of Baltimore was secured in April and Bowes decided to make team management the core of that office's organizational structure and compensation program from the outset. The Indianapolis staff and management heard such good things about the team experience in New York that they did their own research about the feasibility of team management and submitted a team-based reorganization plan to Bowes.

Lessons Learned

Leading corporations such as Motorola, Ford, and General Electric have been using team management to great advantage for nearly a decade. More recently, government and nonprofit organizations have achieved significant improvements in performance and morale through the use of teams. America Works's experience with teams is interesting because although it is a private, for-profit firm that places people in private sector jobs, one segment of its customers is welfare recipients and a major source of its income is in government contracts to move people from welfare to work. The organization's mission to help individuals and families escape poverty through self-sustaining work sounds more like the mission of a nonprofit, charitable organization than that of a profitable, entrepreneurial business.

Team management is working for America Works because teams created a capacity and synergy that exceeded the sum total of the individuals' talents and time taken separately. The team organization also helped renew the spirit and sense of mission and purpose that the staff was losing through frustration with bottlenecks and what they perceived to be management's lack of openness to their ideas for improvement. America Works's team participants were not only more productive and inspired, they were also having fun again, looking forward each morning to coming to the office.

It did not take a long time or cost a great deal of money for America Works to introduce team management. They did decide that they needed outside consultants, but only for a few training sessions and periodic analysis. It did take some extra time for the teams in the early stages, but after a few months, team meetings were short, frequently done "on the fly," and usually resulted in a net savings of work time.

But team management requires a serious commitment from management if it is to succeed. Bowes had to be willing to spend the money for the consultants, to take the risk that the team recommendations would be feasible and responsible, and to spend some money on equipment and training.

America Works is a relatively small, horizontal, entrepreneurial, and privately owned company. It did not need to overcome decades of habit, tradition, or civil service, or layers of bureaucracy. It did not need the permission of the legislature, and it is not accountable to a board of directors or to shareholders. It cannot ignore the media, but it is not subject to freedom of information laws and its compensation plans are not a matter of public record. There are no unions at America Works either.

Bowes was also flexible in her initial experiments with team management. It began as a pilot venture. She selected the initial members but they were not required to participate and membership did change a little over time. She retained ultimate right to approve or veto the team's recommendations, but she did not censor its work. Finally, and perhaps most important, her decision to build the new Baltimore office from the ground up on the principles of team management sent a strong message to all of the offices and to all America Works employees that the team approach had a long-term commitment from the person in charge.

Conclusion

Public managers have a number of tools to use when crafting solutions to public problems. We divide these tools into two categories: *functional tools*, such as budgeting, human resource, and information management, and *innovation tools*, such as reengineering, privatization, and TQM. These distinctions are analytic, and in reality there is considerable overlap among tools. Nevertheless, we find the distinction useful in discussing innovation with practitioners.

We also think of these tools as "strategies of influence." The key job of the manager is to influence organizational behavior. As a manager, you want people to do a better job of solving problems—by better we mean more efficient and more effective. The traditional functional tools remain central to promoting "better" work. If as a manager you want something to happen in an organization, you will need to ensure that resources are available to perform a task. Budgeting, therefore, remains important. At the same time, innovation tools may also enhance the effectiveness of management. For example, it might be possible to leverage someone else's resources to promote the desired end. In this case, the manager should also consider privatization.

Similarly, motivating individual performance is critical to effective human resource management. We have written elsewhere about the importance of targeting incentives to the specific needs of individuals (Cohen and Eimicke, 1995). Most complex tasks in the public sector require team efforts rather than strictly individual performance. Therefore, an emphasis on team management is likely to be a useful addition to standard techniques of human resource management.

Traditional management information systems focus management's attention on meeting specific targets and objectives. Tracking performance is no less critical today than it was in the past.

However, the innovation approach to the use of information as a tool is to conceptualize information management as one element of a more comprehensive system of performance measurement. In addition, by adding benchmarking to your collection of management strategies, you measure and learn from not only your own performance but also the performance of others.

All of these innovation tools can help take you "outside the box" of standard linear thinking and expose you to new ideas and novel ways of looking at a given management challenge. They enhance the effectiveness of traditional management tools while providing for the rapid change required by today's increasingly dynamic organizational environment.

A creative public manager should use all tools that are relevant to the needs of a given situation. The preference for one specific type of tool is too simplistic for a true craftsperson. To be a TQM advocate, a privatization ideologue, or a reengineering zealot strikes us as an ill-informed and narrow-minded approach to organizational management. A carpenter might enjoy using a hammer but will certainly not try to use it when attempting to cut through a two-by-four. Likewise, effective and creative managers must become skilled at applying the appropriate tool to the specific challenge they face.

A Framework for Identifying Appropriate Tools

We acknowledge the limits to the craft and tool metaphors. We know that organizations are more complicated than pieces of wood, and that it is more difficult to implement TQM than to use a hammer. Managers need a framework for identifying the appropriate tool for a given situation. To choose the most appropriate innovation tool, a manager should consider at least the following issues.

- Does the organization have a clear sense of mission? If the answer is no, the manager should consider undertaking a strategic planning process.
- If a clear sense of mission is present, the manager should consider whether the organization has a clear and feasible agenda of tasks designed to achieve that mission. If the answer is yes,

then a strategic plan or its functional equivalent is already in place and such a plan need not be developed.

- Does the organization have effective, agencywide support and production systems, such as personnel and information systems, or a standard set of procedures for tailoring services to meet the specific needs of its customers? If these systems are ineffective, and if the organization has adequate resources and leadership, a reengineering effort might be worth undertaking.
- Does the organization have dissatisfied customers, poor quality, wasteful production processes, and significant amounts of rework? In that case, TQM, and possibly reengineering, is necessary.
- Is the organization's management aware of its current level of performance? If not, the manager should consider improving the organization's measurement systems and integrating them into daily operations.
- When seeking to reengineer or improve production quality, is the organization aware of what its peers have done when facing a similar issue? If not, then benchmarking is worth considering.
- Does the organization have difficulty coordinating the completion of complex tasks efficiently and effectively? If so, team management might be an appropriate tool to apply. The team aspects of TQM might also be appropriate in such a situation.
- Does the organization devote time and resources to tasks that are outside its realm of distinctive or core competency? If so, and if a private market exists or can be created for this service, then privatization might be a reasonable option.

These issues are just a sample of the considerations that the creative public manager must sort through in seeking to identify the innovation tool appropriate in a given situation. Moreover, the answer to the question of what management tool to implement in a situation will vary over time. Management tools can be implemented in a series, or they may be used simultaneously or in combination. A manager might privatize one function, reengineer a second, and assemble a TQM team to address a third. These activities might all be undertaken at once, or as part of a phased-in innovation strategy.

A tremendous advantage to approaching these techniques as tools is that it reduces management's tendency to oversell a particular tool as "the answer." Thinking of management techniques as tools encourages you to analyze each management challenge individually, and then to experiment with different tools until you find the one that is most appropriate. Managers cannot seek scientific answers to definitive questions. Instead, you must look for approximate tendencies, learned through trial and error, to which you can craft a rough but effective solution.

Costs and Benefits of Innovation Tools

Innovation tools must be used situationally, and they must be carefully targeted. One reason for this is that they carry a set of inherent—we would say definitional—costs and benefits. Before using an innovation tool, change agents must assess the organization's capability, environment, and purpose. Next they must understand the costs that a tool may bring. Exhibit C.1 provides a summary of the costs and benefits of the innovation tools analyzed in Chapters Two through Seven. The summary is included here to reinforce the risks that are sometimes involved in using these tools.

Constraints on Using Innovation Tools: Being Realistic

It has taken the better part of the twentieth century to bring the traditional functional tools fully into modern organizational life. The evolution of the modern bureaucratic form of organization is largely the story of adopting rule-driven, and relatively transparent, budget, personnel, information, and reporting systems. It takes time for organizations to learn how to use management tools and to integrate them into the performance of daily tasks. We expect that the innovation tools we have discussed in this book will undergo a similar, although more rapid, evolution and implementation.

Although the demand for rapid change seems obvious, the capacity for such change is limited. Bureaucracy was invented to enshrine predictable, rule-driven, and stable administration. Large-scale organizations were complicated but generally slow to change. As a result, the bureaucratic form effectively decomposed complex tasks into constituent parts and assigned them to specific organizational units. These smaller units then became more expert at the task they had to perform, the program they had to administer, or the client they had to serve. This approach is not effective for organizations that must respond operationally to a rapidly changing environment. The first limit on organizational change in the public sector, therefore, may very well be the bureaucratic form of organization itself.

An advantage of the bureaucratic form for a society governed by a representative democracy is that it sets forth clear chains of command and transparent paths of accountability. The modern interorganizational public sector network involving government, nonprofit contractors, and private firms acting under public policy incentives is necessarily more difficult to control and relatively impossible to "throw out of office." Nevertheless, such networks are custom-made to take advantage of modern production, transportation, and communication technology. Such networks are also more able to use the innovation tools described in this book. To date, government is dominated by old-line bureaucracies rather than by modern interorganizational networks. Although we expect the trend toward network management to accelerate, its relative scarcity is another constraint on the adoption of innovation tools.

A more fundamental constraint is found at the level of the individual. People are attracted to routines. Routines provide us with comfort, confidence, and psychological reinforcement of our competence and ability. In a modern economy characterized by rapid change and, often, pervasive insecurity, people approach demands for new ways of doing work with fear, if not with a nagging sense of the necessity of change. Some individuals are able to develop a positive attitude toward change, while for others the result is quite the opposite.

Even when people embrace change, there is usually a limit on how much and how quickly they can learn to be competent in new organizational routines. Most organizations, but especially public organizations, do not have the luxury of stopping current production while they learn a new way of working. The Environmental Protection Agency (EPA) cannot stop monitoring pollution, the school system cannot stop teaching, and firefighters cannot stop responding to fires. Organizational learning must be accomplished

Exhibit C.1. The Costs and Benefits of Management Innovation.

	Benefits	Costs
Strategic Planning	• A chance for a comprehensive organizational review, identity formation for a new management team, leadership assertion for a chief executive, and articulation of mission and values for wider organizational change.	• Significant expenditures of management time and analytic resources.
	• A shift in focus from immediate tasks to organizational objectives, outputs, and impacts.	• New expectations of massive, rapid change of which the organization may not be capable.
	• New "control," in the sense of helping organizations think.	• New political difficulties that come from exposing the outsider to what an organization is and is not.
Reengineering	• Substantial reductions in cycle time and production costs; increases in productivity and the quality of products and services.	• Expensive outside consulting fees.
		• Little improvement in organizations, and increased employee cynicism.
	• A chance for organizations to take risks, adapt, and change; a new way to take advantage of individual creativity, facilitating organizational survival in	• Frequent disruption of effective, existing processes.
		• Elimination of many middle management jobs, leading many to fear layoffs and jump ship and causing a drop in

the new world of international competition and rapid innovation.

- Changes in work processes because of customer feedback; teams move from being functional to being process-oriented, from performing simple tasks to performing multidimensional ones, from being controlled to being empowered, from basing evaluation and pay on activity to basing them on results, from having protective values to having productive ones.

- organizational spirit among those who remain.
- Potential opposition from every corner of the agency and its concerned advocate community.

TQM

- Transfer of knowledge about work processes from the worker to the organization.
- Empowerment of staff to participate in decisions.
- A potential increase in quality and decrease in production costs as work steps are rationalized and supplies are improved.
- The introduction of customer preferences into an organization, increasing

- Improved production of the wrong thing if the organization's overall strategy is faulty.
- Too much attempted too soon and an effort that will likely fail if standard private sector TQM is applied unmodified in government.
- Possible difficulty in reconciling the claims of competing or contradictory customer demands in the public sector.

Exhibit C.1. (continued)

	Benefits	Costs
	the organization's ability to deliver on them.	• A need for managers to accept significant role changes and a higher degree of risk.
	• The provision of a structured means of eliciting expertise, knowledge, and views in the workplace, without the complications of true workplace democracy.	
Benchmarking and Performance Management	• Ease of understanding and applying the concept.	• Trouble down the road if benchmarking is overly ambitious.
	• Adaptability to a wide range of settings, budgets, and time horizons.	• Subpar outcomes if benchmarks are poorly targeted.
	• No need for extensive or costly training or new equipment.	• An inability to see real performance improvement because of poorly gathered and improperly used information.
	• Support for formation of teams and teamwork.	• Damage to the organization's credibility and reputation if benchmarking is done poorly or dishonestly.
	• More concern for customers, for setting priorities, and for measuring performance on an ongoing basis, with particular emphasis on accountability.	• Discouragement of creativity, ambition, and achievement, and consequently

- Better allocation of organizational resources to meet both long- and short-term goals and responsibilities.

- More "out-of-the-box" thinking, and a constant search for best practices.

Team Management

- The union of people with complementary skills and experiences that exceed the capacity of any one member or the total of individual capacities.

- The ability to respond to a wide variety of challenges from customers, a changing environment, and technological innovation.

- A new understanding of colleagues' work among employees who undergo extensive cross-training, which reduces office segmentation and empowers employees to perform a wider variety of tasks.

- A reduction in barriers between specializations, genders, age groups, races, ethnic groups, and communities.

- reduced likelihood of breakthrough ideas, because of undue focus on others' innovations.

- Inevitable interpersonal conflicts and other obstacles that, if not overcome (through initial training and ongoing access to advice), can waste the organization's resources, hamper morale, and ultimately lead to the organization's demise.

- Necessary revisions of the organization's job descriptions, career ladders, evaluation systems, and office configurations, which may be costly.

- A possible need to reorganize the organization, which would bring the dislocation and expense that come with more traditional restructurings.

Exhibit C.1. (*continued*)

	Benefits	Costs
	• Increased trust and confidence among employees, as well as a stronger commitment to organizational goals. • New incentive for teams to work long, hard, and well, because members enjoy collaborating and achieving more.	
Privatization	• A new possibility of competition in the performance of a public function, which is likely to enhance efficiency and maximize customer choice. • Incentives for managers to keep costs down and improve quality. • New forms of management and technology and new sources of capital. • The possibility of innovation in service delivery. • The possibility of organizational differentiation and focus.	• The loss of direct governmental control over program administration and over the production of goods and services needed to implement public policy. • The government's possible loss of technical expertise or knowledge base with which to manage its private partners effectively. • The need for extra effort, time, and resources devoted to ensuring effective communication between the policy design world and those who will be responsible for implementing the policy.

• A new ability for public managers to focus on policy design, allowing other organizations to worry about the direct administration of government programs.

• A rerouting of national resources toward other sectors of the economy, creating new employment and wealth.

Sale of State-Owned Enterprises

• The expense of establishing management controls and bidding procedures.

• The delegitimization of the government's role in economic development, the loss of the advantages of a mixed economy, and the beginning of the near-worship of the market's glory.

• The possibility of unemployment and social unrest (for example, Treuhandanstalt), which cause human dislocation.

in addition to current tasks. This is also taking place in a period of considerable fiscal constraint. Advocates of organizational learning and change must consider the issue of overload when developing change strategies.

Lessons from the Cases

We have presented cases of innovative public sector organizations managed by the government, managed using the nonprofit form of organization, and operated as a business. The first lesson of these cases is that innovation can take place within all three of these organizational forms. A second lesson is that the three forms of organization are increasingly interacting in the process of delivering public policy and programs.

The New York City Department of Parks and Recreation (DPR) has borrowed TQM and performance tracking from the private sector and applied it to government operations, and it has conducted pilot tests to experiment with privatizing the cleanup and restoration of parks. The Indianapolis Private Industry Council (IPIC) is a nonprofit with an explicit mission of linking private employers with the public welfare system. America Works is a private firm that is paid by government to place welfare recipients into work in other private firms. All three cases provide evidence that the public sector is not just government anymore.

What do these cases teach about management innovation?

• *Leadership is a critical variable.* Goldsmith, Bowes, Gotbaum, and Stern are all strong leaders who had a personal innovation agenda. In each case they committed themselves to success and took risks to achieve superior results.

• *Change is gradual, and failure often precedes success.* America Works failed in Ohio. TQM initially failed at the DPR. Organizations cannot learn new ways of doing things overnight. People make mistakes frequently when they are trying something new. Effective change takes time. Change that is rushed to meet the timetable of a politico on a limited term or of an impatient manager tends to be superficial and short-lived.

• *Innovators use multiple tools.* The DPR used TQM (and then dropped it), strategic planning, performance measurement, and privatization. Mayor Goldsmith used strategic planning, privatization, and reengineering. These approaches illustrate that no single management tool can address all of the needs of a complex organization. Sometimes the right combination of tools is the most effective management innovation of all.

• *Results must be measured.* In the innovation cases there is a heavy emphasis on straightforward measures of outputs and outcomes. For example, the DPR analyzed savings of time and money during the TQM phase, and measures of park cleanliness and conditions in the performance management phase. America Works examined the number of people on welfare successfully placed in private sector jobs.

Critical to the measurement question is an explicit, open definition of the meaning of success. A simple, visible measure to gauge progress toward success and the impact of particular management tools must accompany that clear objective. If team processes are used in America Works and sales double immediately, there is no scientific proof that the team process caused that result. However, a craftsperson might continue in that general direction for a while longer, because the tool seems to be working for now. Correlation is not causality, but without a rigorous measure of an agreed-upon, important result, not even craftlike sensibility can be applied to the problem at hand.

• *Innovation must quickly become commonplace.* Organizations must function within rapidly changing environments. Technological change, increased global trade, and changes in communication, society, politics, and the economy put enormous pressure on organizations in all three sectors (public, private, and nonprofit) to adjust their standard operating procedures to new conditions and stimuli. Global competition means that all organizations must remain aware that the seeds of tomorrow's failure may very well be planted during today's success. In order to thrive, therefore, organizations must embrace change as a way of life.

We believe that the need for innovation and rapid organizational change will be a defining feature of successful organizations in the twenty-first century. The most successful organizations will be those that are able to maintain their mission and distinctive competence while continuously reinterpreting core functions in the light of changed conditions.

• *Standard operating procedures remain important.* Despite the rapidly changing environment, organizations remain collections of coordinated standard operating procedures. As Herbert

Kaufman (1960) saw during his classic study of forest rangers nearly a half a century ago, for an organization to be a conscious, strategic, and managed entity, it must possess preformed responses to specific stimuli.

Standard operating procedures must be redefined, however. No longer can they be mechanical drawings of great detail and specificity. The Forest Service Manual that Kaufman applauded in the 1950s became a mammoth bureaucratic joke by the 1980s. Today, standard operating procedures must act more like modern computer software, providing routines that open pathways and give general direction, rather than as routines that are detailed, rigid directions poured in concrete for all time.

Staff must have the flexibility to work within broad parameters and, every few years or so, to modify the software or architecture itself as changed conditions and new possible responses to old and new conditions emerge. Nevertheless, serious attention must be paid to such organizational software. Standard procedures remain at the heart of all organizations. They define what the organization is and how it will behave. Rapid change and difficult conditions are no excuse for abandoning managed routines. If anything, managers must pay more attention to standard operating procedures because they must now constantly analyze, modify, and relearn them.

The Creative Public Manager

In the past decade we have written about the need for public managers to be more effective, increasingly entrepreneurial, and now, more creative. We have also explicitly broadened the definition of *public manager* to include most of the managers of nonprofit organizations and many managers in the private sector.

Despite the antigovernment rhetoric of the past quarter century, public policy has proven too complex and too important to be left exclusively to government. The innovation tools we have described in this book are not needed because government has been replaced by the majesty of the market. Instead, they are useful because the role of public policy is too central to daily life to leave to government alone.

That seeming paradox is at the heart of the effort to reinvigorate the management of public policy. As the world becomes more urban, as our economic and communication systems become more complex and interconnected, we become more dependent on collective goods for survival. Society cannot afford the inefficiency and ineffectiveness that are sometimes seen in large, bureaucratic organizations. At the same time, critical public policy decisions cannot be left to the vagaries of the market. Hidden hands, massive bureaucratic force, and blunt weapons must be replaced by actions that are more carefully targeted and informed.

Government must use a variety of mechanisms to implement public policy. These include different levels of government, nonprofit organizations, and private organizations. Nongovernmental organizations will require incentives to behave as expected, and the range of expected behavior will necessarily be wider than if government sought to perform these tasks by itself. This means that accountability to representative democratic institutions will be more difficult to achieve. For example, the child welfare agency has less control over a nonprofit contractor than over its own staff. Nevertheless, improved performance measurement with improved communication of information to management can result in more effective performance management and, in the end, a tighter link between public demands and operating public policy.

It is also crucial to understand the risks of more creative, flexible public management. Managers will need to develop new mechanisms of control and influence over implementation. Elected leaders must take time from raising massive amounts of funds from well-heeled contributors and make sure that their constituency relations staff still have the ability to intercede on behalf of the voters. In addition, the risk of corruption is obvious.

If the current rule-laden, bureaucratic system worked well, we might not need to take the risks of more creative, customer-oriented public management. Whether they are called customers or citizens, if people were satisfied with the level of service they receive, there would be no need to reform the current system of public administration. The risks of creative public management are an unfortunate but necessary reflection of the intense, increasing demands we make on public policy.

The modern age requires creative management and innovative management tools. What kind of public manager is required? What do we mean by a creative public manager? Let us return to the craft image. Public managers must fashion solutions to more complex problems, and to do this they need the innovation tools discussed in this book. We should emphasize, however, that these tools can be utilized only by organizations that have the foundation of effective traditional management tools—the reporting, production, and control systems that are ubiquitous in the modern organization.

The creative public manager must be open to new combinations of organizational paths and strategic actions to implement public policy. The creative manager must continuously search for new analogies, and must not be satisfied with an old one simply because it is well understood. People learn by doing and by imitating more experienced practitioners. Until an individual has a mental model of a task, that individual will not be able to perform it. The same is true of how managers approach their work. They begin by looking for the closest example they can find of a similar problem.

When Cohen worked in the EPA's Superfund toxic waste cleanup program, the model built on was the agency's sewage treatment program for "constructing" long-term remedies to toxic pollutants in the land. This approach resulted in toxic waste cleanups built on a model of constructing containment walls and water filtration systems. The agency's oil spill response program was used as a model to develop a way to deal with toxic chemical emergencies. We are not arguing that these are necessarily inappropriate models, but their lineage is a direct reflection of a mental model that senior managers already possessed for other environmental programs.

When Ron Brand began to direct the program to regulate and clean up leaking underground oil and chemical tanks, he had to fight long and hard to avoid using the Superfund model that was present in everyone's mind as he sought to develop a new, more creative design. In his case, the analogy was so powerful it was difficult to resist (Ron Brand, personal communication, March 1992). We are not arguing that creative managers should ignore the past and the lessons that can be derived from it. Rather, we are saying that while very often the old answer is the easy one, it might not be the best one. The creative public manager must look for analogies but must analyze them critically.

The creative public manager cannot insist on total control. He or she must facilitate, leverage, and encourage behaviors rather than command them. Leadership remains critical, but it is a leadership that fully internalizes the need for partnership and collaboration, both inside and outside the organization.

The creative manager must be a lifelong learner. The notion may excite or exhaust you, but it is no longer possible to be successful and coast to an easy victory. In the final analysis, the creative public manager is a hardworking, persistent explorer, not a dilettante artiste. The creative public manager must remain abreast of the way the world is changing, and must acquire the new knowledge needed to continue to serve the public effectively.

Finally, the creative public manager must remain committed to public service and to the ethical values that implies. Innovation is no excuse for amorality or immorality. The goal is to do a better job of serving the public, and to apply all one's ingenuity to that important task. A book on management technique can sometimes communicate by omission. We have not discussed public ethics in this book; therefore, someone might erroneously conclude that we do not believe they are important. Nothing could be further from the truth.

We pursue the study of public management innovation because of our profound belief that there is an ethical imperative to the work of the public sector. The work of the public sector is too important to be left to old methods and outdated technologies. It is also too important to be left to technocrats who do not understand the value and importance of public service and public ethics. Innovation is both feasible and necessary. We believe the ideas in this book can help improve the management of public organizations. By improving public organizations, we can improve public policy and make the world a little better and safer for our children.

References

Ammons, D. *Municipal Benchmarks: Assessing Local Performance and Establishing Community Standards.* Thousand Oaks, Calif.: Sage, 1996.

Amos, N., Cohen, S., and Eimicke, W. *Brooklyn College Quality Education and Service Through Teamwork (BcQuESTT): Evaluation of Completed Projects.* New York: Columbia University Graduate Program in Public Policy and Administration, 1996.

Appelbaum, E., and Batt, R. *The New American Workplace.* Ithaca, N.Y.: Industrial Labor Relations Press, 1987.

Atherton, C., and Windsor, D. "Privatization of Urban Public Services." In C. A. Kent (ed.), *Entrepreneurship and the Privatizing of Government.* Westport, Conn.: Quorum/Greenwood, 1987.

Biesada, A. "Benchmarking." *Financial World,* 1991, *160*(19), 28–32.

Bogan, C., and English, M. J. *Benchmarking for Best Practices.* New York: McGraw-Hill, 1994.

Bowman, J. S. "At Last, an Alternative to Performance Appraisal: Total Quality Management." *Public Administration Review,* 1994, *54*(2), 129–136.

Brecher, C., and Mead, D. M. *Managing the Department of Parks and Recreation in a Period of Fiscal Stress.* New York: Citizens Budget Commission, 1991.

Bruder, K. A., Jr., and Gray, E. M. "Public Sector Benchmarking: A Practical Approach." *Public Manager,* 1994, *76*(9), 9–14.

Bryson, J. M. *Strategic Planning for Public and Nonprofit Organizations.* San Francisco: Jossey-Bass, 1995.

Bryson, J. M., and Roering, W. D. "Strategic Planning Options for the Public Sector." In J. L. Perry (ed.), *Handbook of Public Administration.* San Francisco: Jossey-Bass, 1996.

Champy, J. *Reengineering Management: The Mandate for New Leadership.* New York: HarperCollins, 1996.

Cigler, B. "Adjusting to Changing Expectations on the Local Level." In J. L. Perry (ed.), *Handbook of Public Administration.* San Francisco: Jossey-Bass, 1996.

Cohen, S. *The Effective Public Manager: Achieving Success in Government.* San Francisco: Jossey-Bass, 1988.

Cohen, S., and Brand, R. *Total Quality Management in Government.* San Francisco: Jossey-Bass, 1993.

Cohen, S., and Eimicke, W. "Project-Focused Total Quality Management in the New York City Department of Parks and Recreation." *Public Administration Review, 5*(4), 1994a, 450–456.

Cohen, S., and Eimicke, W. "The Overregulated Civil Service: The Case of New York City's Public Personnel System." *Review of Public Personnel Administration,* spring 1994b, pp. 11–27.

Cohen, S., and Eimicke, W. *The New Effective Public Manager.* San Francisco: Jossey-Bass, 1995.

Cohen, S., and Eimicke, W. *Parks and Recreation as an Essential Municipal Service: The Case of the New York City Department of Parks and Recreation.* New York: Columbia University Graduate Program in Public Policy and Administration, 1996.

Cohen, S., and Eimicke, W. *Welfare to Work: Lessons from Wisconsin, California and Indiana.* New York: Manhattan Institute, spring 1997.

Cohen, S., and Kamieniecki, S. *Environmental Regulation Through Strategic Planning.* Boulder, Colo.: Westview Press, 1991.

Commonwealth Fund. *New Yorkers Say That Upgrading Parks Is Essential to Quality of Life.* New York: Commonwealth Fund, 1994.

Drucker, P. "Reengineering: The Coming of the New Organization." *Harvard Business Review,* Jan.–Feb. 1988, pp. 45–53.

Dunn, C., and others. *Total Quality Management in the New York City Department of Parks and Recreation: Final Report.* New York: Graduate Program in Public Policy and Administration, Columbia University, 1993, p. 1.

Golden, O. "Innovation in Public Sector Human Service Programs: The Implications of Innovation by Groping Along." *Journal of Policy Analysis and Management,* 1990, *9,* 219–248.

Goldsmith, S. "Moving Municipal Services into the Marketplace." Speech delivered at the Carnegie Council Privatization Project, New York, Nov. 20, 1992.

Gore, A. *From Red Tape to Results: Creating a Government That Works Better and Costs Less: Report of the National Performance Review.* Washington, D.C.: U.S. Government Printing Office, 1993.

Grifel, S. S. "Performance Measurement and Budgetary Decisions." *Public Productivity and Management Review,* 1993, *16*(4), 403–407.

Guzzo, R., and Dickson, M. "Teams in Organizations: Recent Research on Performance and Effectiveness." *Annual Review of Psychology,* 1996, *47,* 308.

Hammer, M. "Reengineering Work: Don't Automate, Obliterate." *Harvard Business Review,* July–Aug. 1990, pp. 103–112.

Hammer, M. *Beyond Reengineering.* New York: HarperCollins, 1996.

Hammer, M., and Champy, J. *Reengineering the Corporation: A Manifesto for Business Revolution.* New York: HarperCollins, 1994.

Hammer, M., and Stanton, S. *The Reengineering Revolution: A Handbook.* New York: HarperCollins, 1995.

Hevesi, D. "A Pillar of City Housing: Tax Relief." *New York Times,* Feb. 16, 1997, Real Estate Section, pp. 1, 6.

Hiam, A. *Does Quality Work? A Review of Relevant Studies.* Conference Board, New York City, 1993.

Hofer, C. W., and Schendel, D. E. *Strategy Formulation: Analytical Concepts.* St. Paul, Minn.: West, 1978.

Hudnut, W. H., III. *The Hudnut Years in Indianapolis: 1976 to 1991.* Bloomington: Indiana University Press, 1995.

Hunt, D. *Quality Management for Government: A Guide to Federal, State, and Local Implementation.* Milwaukee: American Society for Quality Control Press, 1993.

International City and County Managers Association. *Measuring the Effectiveness of Basic Municipal Services: Initial Report.* Washington, D.C.: The Urban Institute and the International City and County Managers Association, 1974.

Katzenbach, J., and Smith, D. K. *The Wisdom of Teams: Creating the High-Performance Organization.* Boston: Harvard Business School Press, 1993, pp. 16, 89, 229, 240.

Kaufman, H. *The Forest Ranger: A Study in Administrative Behavior.* Baltimore: Johns Hopkins University Press, 1960.

Kent, C. A. (ed.). *Entrepreneurship and the Privatizing of Government.* Westport, Conn.: Quorum/Greenwood, 1987.

Kent, C. A., and Wooten, S. "Privatizing: The Entrepreneurial Response." In C. A. Kent (ed.), *Entrepreneurship and the Privatizing of Government.* Westport, Conn.: Quorum/Greenwood Books, 1987.

Kettl, D. F. *Sharing Power: Public Governance and Private Markets.* Washington, D.C.: Brookings Institution, 1993.

King, W., and Cleland, D. *Strategic Planning and Policy.* New York: Van Nostrand Reinhold, 1978.

King, W., and Cleland, D. (eds.). *Strategic Planning and Management Handbook.* New York: Van Nostrand Reinhold, 1987.

Kluger, J. "Uncovering the Secrets of Mars." *Time,* July 14, 1997, pp. 27–36.

Koehler, J. W., and Panowski, J. M. *Teams in Government: A Handbook for Team-Based Organizations.* Delray Beach, Fla.: St. Lucie Press, 1996.

Kornblum, W., and Williams, T. "New Yorkers and Central Park: A Report to the Central Park Conservancy," *Evaluation and Policy, Inc.,* April 1983.

Linden, R. *Seamless Government: A Practical Guide to Reengineering in the Public Sector.* San Francisco: Jossey-Bass, 1994.

Makridakis, S., and Héau, D. "The Evolution of Strategic Planning and Management." In W. King and D. Cleland (eds.), *Strategic Planning and Management Handbook.* New York: Van Nostrand Reinhold, 1987.

Mani, B. G. "Old Wine in New Bottles Tastes Better: A Case Study of TQM Implementation in the IRS." *Public Administration Review,* 1995, *55*(2), 147–158.

Mercer, J. L. *Strategic Planning for Public Managers.* Westport, Conn.: Quorum/Greenwood, 1991.

Meyersohn, R. "Van Cortlandt Park and Pelham Bay Park and their Visitors, 1986–87: A Report Prepared for the City of New York Department of Parks and Recreation," Center for Social Research, Graduate School and University Center of the City University of New York, 1987.

Micklethwait, J., and Wooldridge, A. *The Witch Doctors: Making Sense of the Management Gurus.* New York: Random House, 1996.

Mintzberg, H. *The Rise and Fall of Strategic Planning.* New York: Free Press, 1994.

Morgan, C., and Murgatroyd, S. *Total Quality Management in the Public Sector: An International Perspective.* Bristol, Pa.: Open University Press, 1994.

National Academy of Public Administration. *Reengineering for Results: Keys to Successful Government Experience.* Washington, D.C.: National Academy of Public Administration, Aug. 1994.

Newland, C. "The National Government in Transition." In J. L. Perry (ed.), *Handbook of Public Administration.* San Francisco: Jossey-Bass, 1996.

New York City. *Adopted Budget, Fiscal Year 1995.* New York: 1995.

New York City Department of Parks and Recreation. *Eight Seasons: A Report to the People.* New York: New York City Department of Parks and Recreation, 1996a.

New York City Department of Parks and Recreation. *Parks Inspection Program Internal Documents.* New York: Department of Parks and Recreation, 1996b.

Osborne, D., and Gaebler, T. *Reinventing Government: How the Entrepreneurial Spirit Is Transforming the Public Sector.* Reading, Mass.: Addison-Wesley, 1992.

Osborne, D., and Plastrik, P. *Banishing Bureaucracy: The Five Strategies for Reinventing Government.* Reading, Mass: Addison-Wesley, 1997.

Parker, G. M. *Team Players and Teamwork.* San Francisco: Jossey-Bass, 1996.

Parkhurst, D. "A New Way for Arlington County." *Public Innovator,* June 16, 1994, p. 5.

Parks Council and Central Park Conservancy. *Public Space for Public Life: A Plan for the Twenty-First Century.* New York: Parks Council and Central Park Conservancy, 1993.

Peters, T. *Liberation Management.* New York: Fawcett, 1992.

Praeger, J. "Contracting Out Government Services: Lessons from the Private Sector." *Public Administration Review,* 1994, *54*(2), 176–184.

Protzman, F. "East Nearly Privatized, Germans Argue the Cost." *New York Times,* Aug. 12, 1994, p. D1.

Pugh, D. S., and Hickson, D. H. *Writers on Organization.* Thousand Oaks, Calif.: Sage, 1989.

Rodkey, G. "Saving Time and Money in Washington." *Public Innovator,* Dec. 15, 1994, pp. 4–5.

Rothman, H., and Scott, M. *Companies with a Conscience.* New York: Birch Lane Press, 1992.

Sanger, M. B., and Levin, M. A. "Using Old Stuff in New Ways: Innovation as a Case of Evolutionary Tinkering." *Journal of Policy Analysis and Management,* 1992, *11*(1), 88–115.

Savas, E. *Privatizing the Public Sector: How to Shrink Government.* Chatham, N.J.: Chatham House, 1982.

Savas, E. *Privatization: The Key to Better Government.* Chatham, N.J.: Chatham House, 1987.

Scholtes, P. (ed.). *The Team Handbook.* (2nd ed.) Madison, Wis.: Joiner Associates, 1996.

Schuckel, K. "Poll Respondents Want Welfare Funds Used Wisely." *Indianapolis Star,* Apr. 21, 1996, pp. B1, B7.

Sutherland, J. W. (ed.). *Management Handbook for Public Administrators.* New York: Van Nostrand Reinhold, 1978.

Swiss, J. E. "Adapting Total Quality Management (TQM) to Government." *Public Administration Review,* 1992, *52*(4), 356–362.

Taylor, B. "An Overview of Strategic Planning." In W. King and D. Cleland (eds.), *Strategic Planning and Management Handbook.* New York: Van Nostrand Reinhold, 1987.

Ukeles Associates, Inc. *The Users of Riverside Park.* New York: Riverside Park Fund, 1991.

Van Oudenhoven, J. P. "Privatization in Europe." In L. Finley (ed.), *Public Sector Privatization.* Westport, Conn.: Quorum/Greenwood, 1989.

Walters, J. "The Benchmarking Craze." *Governing,* Apr. 1994a, pp. 33–37.

Walters, J. "TQM: Surviving the Cynics." *Governing,* Sept. 1994b, pp. 40–45.

Walton, M. *The Deming Management Method.* New York: Perigree Books, 1986.

Index